£3

*GOD'S SCOTLAND?*

# GOD'S
## SCOTLAND?

THE STORY OF SCOTTISH CHRISTIAN RELIGION

Compiled by
## Anne Pagan

Preface by
## Andrew Monaghan

RADIO
FORTH
Close to you

MAINSTREAM
PUBLISHING

Copyright © Radio Forth, 1988

All rights reserved
First published in Great Britain in 1988 by
MAINSTREAM PUBLISHING COMPANY
(EDINBURGH) LTD

7 Albany Street, Edinburgh EH1 3UG

ISBN 1  85158  150  2 (paper)

No part of this book may be reproduced or transmitted in any form or by
any other means without the permission in writing from the publisher,
except by a reviewer who wishes to quote brief passages in connection
with a review written for insertion in a magazine, newspaper or
broadcast.

**British Library Cataloguing in Publication Data**
Pagan, Anne
 God's Scotland?
 1. Scotland. Christian church, to 1983
 I. Title
 274.11

Cover illustration of Iona Cross by permission of the Scottish Tourist Board

Typeset in 11/13 Imprint by Bookworm Typesetting Ltd, Edinburgh.
Printed in Great Britain by Billings & Sons, Worcester.

Anne Pagan presents 'View from Earth', the weekly religious magazine programme on Radio Forth, and has shared the awards this programme has won for its innovative programming and imaginative treatment of issues of interest, not only for a religious but for a general audience. Born a 'Falkirk bairn', she now lives with her husband Jim and her two teenage sons in Edinburgh. At present she works part-time in the library of the University of Edinburgh but is a qualified and experienced primary school teacher. She is part of the team from the Edinburgh and District Churches' Council for Local Broadcasting which works with Radio Forth to give a broad base in the churches to controversial projects such as this rewriting of Scottish church history.

# CONTENTS

# ACKNOWLEDGEMENTS

Both the series on Radio Forth and this book were only made possible by the research and generous co-operation of the following list of contributors:

Bernard Aspinwall, University of Glasgow
Dr John W.M. Bannerman, University of Edinburgh
Dr Frank Bardgett, Church of Scotland minister
Professor Geoffrey W.S. Barrow, University of Edinburgh
Dr Callum G. Brown, University of Strathclyde
Professor Alex. C. Cheyne, former principal of New College
Dr Tristram Clarke, Scottish Record Office
Professor Ian B. Cowan, University of Glasgow
Rev. Mark Dilworth, Archivist of the Roman Catholic Church
Dr John Durkan, University of Glasgow
Dr William Ferguson, University of Edinburgh
Ian Fisher, RCAHMS
Dr Mary Furgol, now living in the United States of America
Dr Thomas Gallagher, University of Bradford
Dr John Hedges, University of Oxford
Peter Hills, Director of Whithorn Archaeological Dig
Dr Christine Johnston, Archivist to Lothian Health Board
Dr Michael Lynch, University of Edinburgh
Dr Walter Makey, former Edinburgh City Archivist
Dr Roger Mason, University of St Andrews
Dr Donald Meek, University of Edinburgh
Dr Anna Ritchie, Secretary to the Society of Antiquaries
Dr Graham Ritchie, RCAHMS
Dr Andrew C. Ross, New College
Dr Margaret H.B. Sanderson, Scottish Record Office
Dr Duncan Shaw, Church of Scotland minister
Dr Murray Simpson, Librarian of New College
Professor T.C. Smout, University of St Andrews
Dr David Stevenson, University of Aberdeen
Dr Jenny Wormald, St Hilda's College, Oxford

# FOREWORD

This book emerged from the co-operation of Radio Forth, the production team of the Edinburgh and District Churches' Council for Local Broadcasting and the Scottish History Department of the University of Edinburgh. I was privileged to produce the radio series, 'The Story of Scottish Religion', which gave birth to the book.

I have always been interested in Scottish history, but working with the Scottish History Department has made me not a little envious of the young people who study with them. Research into Scottish history is a fascinating and challenging area which to me is making up for lost time in the developing work taking place in the Department. Meeting their colleagues throughout Scotland and beyond brought home to me that the vitality of the research extends through the universities and into the archaeological and palaeographical institutions. It has been a refreshing experience.

Clearly a small book like this cannot do justice to all the strands in Scottish religion, not even within the mainstream Christian religion covered by this book. Each Christian insight into Scotland's past and present contributes to the Christian faith and experience, both of those who commit themselves to it and those who only see it as a formative element in modern Scotland. Modern Scotland, too, is enriched by the religious traditions of so many other faiths: but that is another book! I apologise unreservedly in advance to those who feel their experience has not been given due weight and can only say no judgment is involved in the weighting.

What is of value in this book stems from the academics who have given so generously of their time (and particularly Dr Michael Lynch of the University of Edinburgh). A list of the contributors is given and I would like to thank them individually. I would also like to thank Joan Oswald who conducted the radio interviews with indefatigable energy and organisation. Without her, or Anne Pagan, the book would have remained an idea. Without the constant encouragement of Radio Forth management, even the idea might not have seen the light of day.

*Andrew Monaghan*

# I OUR ANCESTORS

## 1 The story of mainstream Scottish religion – before Christ

'Tell me a story' is not just a child's repeated request to its parents. It's also what we all look for as human beings and there's no more fascinating story than that of mainstream Scottish Christian religion. William Cantwell Smith – after a great deal of heart-searching and research – defined religion as having two elements. The first is a historical cumulative tradition: and so we'll look at all the bits and pieces building up in the story of mainstream Scottish religion. The second is the personal faith of men and women: and this, too, we'll be speaking about – the story of men and women from St Ninian through the great characters of the Reformation age right up to those who shaped the issues we still face today in modern Scotland, where only one in ten might go to church but where nine out of ten still see themselves as religious.

The story of men and women in Scotland goes back some seven thousand years before Christ. One of the most popular misconceptions has been that people at that stage were really small: in fact they were only a little smaller than ourselves and were equipped with trades, crafts and skills showing that they were a lot more sophisticated than we gave them credit for. The earliest real evidence, however, only goes back to 4,000 years before Christ. We know little of the earliest fishermen who came ashore and settled down and so we know little of their religion. All we can do is reflect on the fascinating evidence of the archaeologists and then compare and contrast the facts that lie beneath the folk traditions in this country, the beliefs known of elsewhere and the continuing symbolisms that were adopted in Christian decorative art from the flourishing crafts that went before. The vestiges of pagan worship – such as children dancing naked round the maypole and fertility rites for spring and harvest – which went on as aberrations in the medieval church in the odd rural parish, challenge us to attempt to trace

2

back the layers of Christianisation of such ritual to explore the fears, the superstitions and the searchings that were those of more primitive people. The freshness of their response to nature and the mystery of life may well sharpen up our own understanding of what goes on underneath the cultivated and often superficial veneer of twentieth-century relationships.

We don't have in Scotland anything so impressive as the combined evidence of Tacitus, the Roman historian, and the archaeological finds at Windeby in Germany and Tolland in Denmark which relate respectively to a girl ritually executed for immorality and a man sacrificed to a god or goddess. That sort of find gave theologians something to get working on. Not so in Scotland, but there are starting-off points. At a much later date, we do know from Adomnán that the Picts of the sixth century had important pagan priests. In the light of that fact, we then look at the archaeological evidence of careful, highly organised communal funeral rituals on sites 2,500 years before Christ. The next stage is to test out the hypothesis that there were priests in that society against the pattern of similar societies we know more about and against every fact we can discover on sites like Maes Howe and the other great Orkney sites. We do so always on the principle that looking back may well enrich our understanding of ourselves today.

Stone circle and alignments, Callanish, Lewis (*by permission of the Royal Commission on the Ancient and Historical Monuments of Scotland*)

3

## 2  Death, sun and moon

Maes Howe – the Neolithic passage grave so many people visit in the Orkneys – is one of the wonders of the prehistoric world. It's incomparable in its graceful architecture and ritual symbolism, evidencing to some sort of meeting between the worship of the moon as seen in the recumbent stone circles of the north-east and the worship of the sun. On 21 November 1972, the evening of the winter solstice, the Orcadian author George Mackay Brown and a few friends waited inside the great chamber. As the sun descended, it came right through the tomb and, as he puts it, 'the sunset flowered on the stone – the last beam of light of the shortest day – and it glowed briefly on a wall that at every other time of the year is dark'. A long controverted theory had been proved: it could have been no accident but rather a matter of careful design and knowledge. It is the evidence of careful design as exposed in the painstaking excavations and cataloguing of the sort of people we talked to for the series, people like Audrey Henshall, Graham and Anna Ritchie, Liz Thoms and John Hedges, that are only now – after the hundred years' work that preceded them – building the elements which will allow us in the future to say something about primitive religion.

The study is important because, in every area of the world, Christianity has always been shaped by the situation in which it takes root: otherwise it dies. Much more hard work will have to be done before we can find really helpful clues to understand our religious past and maximise the hidden content of our own particular Scottish religious insights.

That all sounds very grand but the foundations are more matter of fact. Our ancestors built immensely sophisticated chamber tombs which were used again and again for burials between 4,000 and 2,000 BC. Then we tend to find more evidence of individual burials of more important persons: some with magnificent possessions, mead in vessels and meadow

4

flowers, which raise questions of primitive searchings for a future life with food for the journey. Most of the evidence, however, is of reverence for ancestors as a stretching out into the unknown and a very fearful desire to continue successful farming practices by identification with the ways and being of those who went before. Territorial divisions and structures in society are marked out by the burial patterns and we only glimpse a society that is both immensely practical and religiously and socially sensitive. Skara Brae – preserved so amazingly beneath the sand – is a whole village where the uniformity of even the stone furniture witnesses to a sophisticated society. Cairnpapple in West Lothian shows on one site successive burial patterns imposed one on another with different beliefs underlying those patterns. People were clearly searching both as individuals and, as the ritual circles at Stenness and Brodgar indicate, witnessing to that searching in ceremonies that look at death, nature and the sky of sun and moon – the uncertainties of life that are with us still.

Standing stones, Callanish, Lewis (*by permission of the Royal Commission on the Ancient and Historical Monuments of Scotland*)

## 3   Skulls, totems and eagles

The story here begins at Isbister in Orkney with a farmer out on the flagstones on the shore looking for flat stone. What he found was one of the richest collections of Neolithic treasures: axes, a button of jet and a stone knife. Careful excavation on his own initiative was to follow – and we now have a whole series of windows into the religious life of our ancestors of 5,000 years ago. When the Norse chapels were built, they were built on these settlements and, some experts believe, even on the holy places of old, providing a continuity right through to many of the parishes of today in physical location. That is a fascinating area of research but more important are the ideas that challenged then and still challenge us in different ways today. The sociologists would say religion comes in to explain and perhaps give some power over the things that lie beyond man's control. It also reinforces social structures and taboos. From the evidence of Isbister, it's clear that the reality of the highly developed social structure of the Neolithic peoples in this world was closely associated with their imaginings about the next world. What's fascinating about modern research into present-day attitudes is that even among religious people, there is a parallel confusion about eternal life and social structures. Beliefs perhaps don't change that much after all!

The Isbister tomb had bodies placed in it for only about a hundred years but was then used for burial rituals for another 800 more. It wasn't that people were buried in it but their bodies were hung outside until bare of flesh and then only some of the bones were buried, presumably at special ceremonial times in these tombs that marked both their territory and their belonging. There are remains of sacrifices of food offered to the tomb not to the individuals – presumably to gain good harvests. The organisation of it all around central points with deposits of bones at Isbister and elsewhere in Orkney would seem to demand the existence of priests as intermediaries between the people and the other world they wished to stay in touch with. Who were their gods? We don't know, is the short answer. We don't know if the moon worship meant female gods and female priestesses or if it was always male dominated, as seems at times to be the case with sun worship. The deities were certainly related to the uncertainties of nature and the seasons. On the principle that they would reflect the structures of the sophisticated tribal society they emerged from, Dr John Hedges of the University of Oxford suggests that they would have had a hierarchy of gods reflecting the myth stories of creation that mark most if not all similar cultures. Ancestors were important and may well have been regarded as lesser gods at some stages of the ebb and flow of tribal development. Each group seems to have had its own totemic symbol to represent its identity, to be reverenced and to stand for its wish to be linked with the great unknown that was the unity of life beyond its limitations. In Isbister, that totemic symbol was the great white-tailed eagle with all its associations – at least in our thinking today – of power, majesty and the freedom of the open skies. A sense of wonder doesn't go wrong, even in the technological age!

Chambered cairn, Isbister, Orkney (*by permission of J.W. Hedges*)

## 4 Druids – priests of fear or thinkers?

Research has shown many animal and human sacrifices in every previous age of history of which we have information: on the Scottish scene we have little evidence. Going back to 2,500 years before Christ, Dr John Hedges of the University of Oxford gives us in his account of the Isbister tomb a vivid picture of skulls rolled into a chamber and detailed accounts of thousands of animal sacrifices in the tomb. At the standing stones, bodies were buried but we don't know if these were founding sacrifices as in other parts of the world. In later times skulls were reverenced in Scotland including horned and triple-headed ones: again a normal indication of human sacrifice. Two thousand years after Isbister, we meet the Celts who ranged across Europe in a pattern marked by the rather frightening cult of the severed head: thus the Salii at Entremont in Provence and Roquepertuse in Bouches-du-Rhone. The period from the birth of Christ until the coming of Christianity to Scotland was the era of the Celts: Scots, Britons and Picts. Here we have Roman writers like Strabo witnessing to the prevalence of human sacrifice but in Scotland Dr Anna Ritchie, Secretary to the Society of Antiquaries, maintains that there is no evidence of human sacrifice in the time of the Picts. This doesn't mean there wasn't human sacrifice, of course, since such human sacrifice doesn't normally have lasting memorials erected for the victims, but there are no real grounds for tying together all the traces in Scotland's prehistory into a confrontation between primitive fear-filled religion and the coming of Christianity. What we do know is that the Picts, for example, spoke mainly a form of Celtic (P-Celtic) and also at least one other non-Indo-European language in which the few later unintelligible Pictish Ogam inscriptions were written. These and other elements of Scots and Pictish life open up links with wider Celtic and pre-Celtic culture and a religion based on reverence for the earth, for water (witness the traditional holy wells), for animals and for a divine organisation of gods that mirrored their own society: a father-figure at the top (Dagoda among the Scots), and female sexual deities of fertility and Lugh (whom the Romans equated with Mercury). There were four great festivals with Samhain as the greatest on 31 October, the feast of death and new life Christianised later into Hallowe'en.

At the centre of this faith were the Druids. Julius Caesar gives us long detailed descriptions of them. The Vates offered sacrifices but Caesar witnesses clearly to the fact that Druids were essentially philosophers and teachers. We know that those in southern Britain went for years of study to the continent so we can presume that the northern Druids were just as learned. Their place in society was an honoured, influential one, between the king and the freemen in centres like Inverness and presumably Traprain Law in East Lothian. They believed in an after-life so clearly that they were willing to make repayments of loans in death because everyone would be there after death. Their rituals centred on oak groves: and our Christmas mistletoe (which grows on oak) was originally reverenced as one of the many sources of natural magic, bringing both joy and fear in different rituals. As is clear in Adomnán's *Life of Columba*, magi or Druids were in a central role in Pictish society, ready to debate the claims of the Christian faith. The account of Columba's meeting with King Bridei's magus is 'glorified' but witnesses to a very real meeting of Christ's claims with the religious power-base of the Celts; both were to shape the distinctive patterns of Celtic Christianity.

# II THE FIRST TEN CENTURIES

## 5 The Romans are coming!

It must have been an awesome sight for the Britons of the great fortified villages like Traprain Law to see the march of the Roman legions who invaded Scotland under Agricola from AD 78 to 85. By the end of AD 83, he had established a line of forts between the Forth and the Clyde driving into Scotland by land and sea and from east and west. The fort of Trimontium at Newstead on the River Tweed (opposite another tribal stronghold on the Eildon Hills) was one of the main power-bases for the operation. The decisive battle was at Mons Graupius, probably in Aberdeenshire, when Tacitus says 10,000 of the enemy were killed. The fleet even subdued the Orkneys and saw the Shetlands (Thule) which were considered to be the end of the earth. The invaders had to fall back to Hadrian's Wall (built in 120-128) but a relatively stable period took place when the Antonine Wall was built in 142-143 and lasted for about forty to fifty years. 'The Romans are coming' meant that the old gods had to give way first to the Roman gods and then to Christianity. Tradition has it that Pomponia Graecina, wife of Aulius Plautius, the first Roman commander in AD 43, was a Christian but the first administrative network was linked with that of the Roman pantheon of gods: Jupiter, Mars, Mercury, Apollo and Fortuna, as well as local versions: Brigantia, Brittania, Cocidius and Maponus. Jupiter Dolichenus (Eastern) was worshipped at Croy Hill while German deities are found at Birrens and Cramond. One of the tragedies in investigating this period was the destruction in 1743 of a Roman temple, Arthur's O'on (or Oven) near Camelon. It was built as a trophy to commemorate a victory and was a circular beehive-shaped building about six metres tall.

As the Roman Empire became Christian so the scattering of Christians in Roman Britain was rather dramatically increased. In 209, Tertullian (in North Africa) wrote, 'Those parts of Britain where the Romans had no access are subject to Christ.'

This could only have been Scotland but at most his statement can only be taken as a pointer to there being some Christians in Scotland outside the direct sphere of Roman administration. By the fourth century, there was an organised church in the Roman province of Britain. It sent no less than three bishops to the Council of Arles (314) and the Council of Rimini (359) (one of them accompanied by a priest and a deacon). Three martyrs (including St Alban) were claimed in the Diocletian persecution (300) and St Athanasius praised Britons for their role in the worldwide Arian controversy (they were on the right side). When the Roman Empire became officially Christian (380), it was weakening in Britain but we know of one great scholar, Pelagius (eventually an unwitting heretic), who went from Britain to a scholarly and influential role in the wider church around the turn of the century (400). Scotland was part of this whole process, at least in the area south of the Antonine Wall: the Christian 'chi-rho' (℞) symbol appeared with regularity. The Christian church here remained integrated in faith, worship and institutions with Rome, the centre of the church even when the power of the empire was broken. It was based on the territorial organisation of the Roman province with the *civitas* or urban centre and associated rural area becoming the bishop's see and diocese. The old myth of a different type of kirk in Scotland from the rest of Europe at this time is only that, a myth. It was very much conscious of and respected as part of the one, holy, Roman and Catholic church.

## 6 Ninian and Whithorn: early Christianity in the south-west

The 'Whithorn Dig' has in recent years focused attention on the picturesque village of Whithorn on the northern shores of the Solway Firth – and on the shadowy figure of Ninian. In the past, excavations at the chapel on the Isle of Whithorn found no evidence of early occupation whereas those on Ardwall Isle (of the Isles of Fleet) showed at least three Celtic foundations and cemeteries of different periods. Whithorn Priory unearthed very primitive coffins and revealed white plaster on a primitive building, though not one early enough to substantiate the tradition that Ninian built a *Candida casa*, a white house in the Roman manner (perhaps a lime-coloured stone building). The present excavations seem to show three major stages of development: an early Christian settlement of the fourth century which at the time of writing has only been glimpsed; a later more developed site with many buildings of the fifth and sixth centuries; and a Viking trading post of the tenth or eleventh centuries.

Where Ninian fits into those Christian settlements is far from clear. Bede in his *Historia Ecclesiastica* (c.731) writes of Ninian and presumably is giving the local tradition derived from his friend Pechthelm, the contemporary Anglian bishop of *Candida casa* at Whithorn. From this and other scanty evidence (much of which has to be layered away out of more 'miraculous' and politically motivated versions and traditional place names), we know that Ninian was a Briton (perhaps from the early community we glimpse in the excavations) who was trained in Gaul and must also have been at least an admirer of St Martin of Tours and his spirituality since the church at Whithorn came to be dedicated to him. He came back to Whithorn as bishop in the Roman and continental style of church government. Whithorn then was a British foundation and Peter Hills, Director of the Whithorn Archaeological Dig, makes it clear that his recent archaeological finds point clearly to British influence and not the later Irish Catholic tradition that is based on the monastic structure. There is no sign of the typical Celtic church *vallum* and the buildings are rectangular and not circular as in Irish monasticism. Signs of monastic life do exist at the earlier level, in particular the man-made earth beds for the monastery garden and split tree-trunk coffins which parallel those found in Armagh in Patrick's foundation.

As for Ninian's dates, there are real disagreements. Bede's dating would place him around 400 but most people would now place him later, possibly from 450 to 500 or even 550. Dr John Bannerman of the University of Edinburgh emphasises that a date about the middle of the fifth century is now likely but that the suggestions that he was as late as the sixth century are ruled out by the wider historical context. Yet another controversy centres on claims that Ninian converted some of the southern Picts. A statement by Patrick to Coroticus and indications in some late documents seemed to have been discredited but sophisticated name analysis and other modern techniques have reaffirmed the view that Ninian was active among the southern Picts as well as on the northern shores of the Solway. Ninian's importance and influence were to be upstaged by the Columban tradition but Whithorn became a centre of pilgrimage in the twelfth century when the search was on for a saint who was free of Celtic church associations. Ninian may yet have a great deal to tell us – and teach us about the Christian religion in Scotland.

Whithorn Priory, Wigtownshire (*by permission of the Royal Commission on the Ancient and Historical Monuments of Scotland*)

## 7  Patrick – what's he got to do with Scotland?

The name Patrick is synonymous today with Ireland but there are two reasons why he has an important place in the story of the church in Scotland. The first is that he brought Christianity to the Scots of Northern Ireland from his bishop's see at Armagh: and these were the Scots who crossed the north channel, many of them as Christians, to found the Scottish kingdom of Dalriada in the West of Scotland. The second intriguing reason is that Patrick was a Briton born of a *decurio*, one of the governing class in Roman provincial society and a deacon of the church. He tells us he was born at Banavem Taberniae which may have been anywhere on the south-west coast of Scotland or Wales – probably Scotland if only because he operated in the north of Ireland. Patrick's dates are controverted. Traditionally, it's thought he was born in 389 and active from 432 to 461 as bishop of Armagh; but the *Annals of Ulster* would have his work a generation later, with his death nearer 493. This is the latest possible date for him but significantly is still before the critical date for the establishment of the Irish Scots in Dalriada which is *c*.500, when King Fergus Mor moved his base to Scotland. Thus the Scots coming in waves into Scotland would also be bringing the Christian faith.

We have a clear idea of many things about Patrick from two documents he left behind, his 'Confession of Faith' and his 'Letter to Coroticus'. In his Confession, he appears as a humble man of prayer who came through incredible hardships to achieve immense long-term achievement for Christianity in Ireland. When he was sixteen, Scots pirates from Ireland raided his father's home and it was during six years as a slave that he deepened his character and spirituality. He escaped, visited his parents and studied on the continent to become a priest so that he could go back to bring Christianity to the Scots who had enslaved him. Despite opposition from family, friends and 'the elders' of the church because of his lack of literary skills, he had what he calls 'the fear of God (reverential) as the guide of my journey through Gaul, Italy and the islands of the Tyrolene Sea'. Eventually, he went to Ireland as bishop and, in the absence of a suitable *civitas* (or city) on the Roman model, established his see at Armagh beside the great Ulster stronghold of Emain Macha. He longed to visit his parents again but never managed to do so: his amazing missionary work, however, ensured his influence spread back to his mainland birthplace.

A final intriguing window into the early story of Christianity in Scotland is provided by his 'Letter' to Coroticus, king of the Britons of Strathclyde, upbraiding him for invading Ireland and enslaving some of Patrick's converts by his band of 'mercenaries, heathen Scots and apostate Picts'. Much speculation surrounds this last phrase for it normally refers to Christians who've abandoned their faith. Some have argued that apostate is mere invective but on balance Patrick's words do seem to link, in the context of the other evidence, to the

likelihood that Ninian's work did indeed bring Christianity to some of the Picts at an earlier date. Be that as it may, since the Scots were finally to take over from the Picts, Patrick's influence is in any view a vital one and places like Kirkpatrick and dedications throughout Scotland – right across to Gullane in the east – witness to that.

Pictish symbol stone, Pabay graveyard, Inverness-shire (*by permission of the Royal Commission on the Ancient and Historical Monuments of Scotland*)

## 8 Bridget – saint and goddess rolled into one?

In the person of St Bridget (also in the form of Brigit, Bride and Brighde), we meet not only the saint with the most dedications in Scotland but also a person who strikingly illustrates the way the meeting of Christianity and Celtic religion led to a triumph for Christianity in the important issues and a triumph for Celtic imagery and poetry in the distinctive Scottish and Irish expression of Christianity. For dedications, think of all the Kilbrides, Kirkbrides, and Bridekirks; but also Abernethy – founded by the abbess of Kildare in the seventh century – Blair Atholl and Pitlimbertie in Fife. The story of Bridget illustrates that the Christian church, in becoming rooted at the heart of Gaelic life, either respected the accidentals and the customs or found itself unable to change them. Until very recently, the residents of Colonsay kept a Candlemas custom called Bride's bed. A sheaf of corn in the shape of a woman and a wooden club were put in a basket into the fire at night. Woe betide the harvest if there were no imprint of club in the ashes in response to their chant 'Bride is come, Bride is welcome'. Right through Scotland, Bride is the centre of sentimental stories, songs and customs.

The real St Bridget, who died about 524, founded the double monastery for monks and nuns at Kildare which is one of the earliest centres for the monasticism which was to prove in time so suited to the Irish and Scottish situations that it came to provide the organisational structure within which bishops exercised their spiritual ministry. Her story is told by Cogitosus a century and a half later but it was already inextricably linked with her namesake, the Celtic Brigit, goddess daughter of the great Dagoda, Lord of the earth. She was a fire-goddess and so we find Cogitosus noting that in Kildare monastery at his time the nuns still guarded her sacred fire. The name Kildare means the church of the oak tree: Druid and oak tree have the same word root and the most striking of ritual associations. Kildare then seems in the usual pattern to have been a pagan sanctuary before the Christian 'holy place' took over.

There are legends that Bridget was consecrated bishop by mistake (women's rights campaigners take note!) but what is certain is that she has been accurately described as the Gael's Virgin Mary. She was presented as *Muime Chriosd*, Christ's foster-mother, in the kin-based society that was Gaeldom. The foster-mother role was even stronger than that of the natural mother and such children lived with their foster-parents. It's an interesting pattern for Christian ideals of foster-parenting in our own modern society but also a remarkable testimony to the honoured place of women in the monastic system and in the emerging Celtic church. The fact that she's still associated with superstitious fertility rites as well as crosses blessed at mass for the newly-sown crops shouldn't blind us to the serious and intriguing questions she raises about the integration of Celtic culture into a Christianity that affected every aspect of everyday life. Christianity today is too often accused of being out of touch with real life: not so the faith of our ancestors, warts and all, saints and goddesses alike!

## 9  Monastic church – the uniqueness of the Celtic church

The special character of the Celtic church arose from the dramatic rise of the importance of monastic life and the way it both developed Celtic culture and became also the organisational structure of the Celtic church.

The story begins in Egypt in the third century when persecution of Christians by Rome encouraged the flight into the desert which had already been seen from the Old Testament prophets and Christ Himself when he was preparing for his life's work as a way of getting close to God. Via Gaul, Christianity came to Ireland by way of Antony and Pachomius from Egypt and then the Greek and Frankish monks, Basil and Cassian; it was marked by its strictness and took both the form of the hermit's life and the more community-based form which gathered the hermits together for prayer and the development of learning. This was its first importance in Ireland and Scotland. The word for desert moved into Gaelic as hermitage, as can be seen in the story of St Serf in Dysart in Fife. He appears in the sixth century as Kentigern's teacher, and St Serf's island monastery in Loch Leven shows his enduring in that area. The hermitage and the monastery inherited the role of preserving and building Gaelic literature from the professional caste of poets and story-tellers, many of whom were recruited for the spreading of the Christian faith. They were the media men of their time and their partnership with the new faith meant a rather unique blend of asceticism, giving up the world, with the Gaelic lyric poetry of the beauty of nature. It stands out like a beacon from the Dark Ages. Thus a ninth-century Gaelic poem: 'the little bird that has whistled from the point of a bright yellow bill, it utters a note above Loch Laoigh, a blackbird from a yellow heaped branch'.

The other unique aspect of the Celtic church arose from circumstances. The Roman structure of bishops and dioceses (modelled on the Roman Empire), as established by Ninian in

Scotland and Patrick in Ireland, rapidly gave way to a church of monasteries much more suited to the kin-based and wholly rural society of Scotland and Ireland. The bishop, priest and deacon were present just as they were in the Roman church but they were first and foremost monks and as such under the jurisdiction of the abbot. In other words, whereas the bishop was the sole authority in the Roman or continental church, there were two heads in the Celtic church: the bishop for spiritual matters, the abbot for temporal administration. It was possible for one man to hold both offices but Columba himself did not become a bishop because he felt unworthy; bishops took the place of honour in the liturgy of the mass even with him. As Dr John Bannerman of the University of Edinburgh stresses, the important thing to get right about this process is that it does not imply the Celtic church and the Roman church were two different churches. People of the period would have been horrified at the suggestion. Rome was just as much the spiritual centre of the Celtic church as any other; the diversity of organisational structure – despite odd hiccups when war made communication difficult, as with the date of Easter and the shape of the tonsure – may well, however, have lessons for the movement to unity in the Christian churches today. Unity need not mean uniformity.

Kildalton Cross, Islay
(*by permission of the Royal Commission on the Ancient and Historical Monuments of Scotland*)

## 10   Columba and Iona – vision and energy rediscovered

Columba and the monastic tradition he established on Iona are central to the past history of the Christian faith in Scotland and – with the renewed vision found on Iona by George MacLeod – an inspiration for today. His Gaelic name *Colum Cille* means 'dove of the church', hence the Latin *columba*, the dove of peace. Lord George MacLeod in the thirties and after the war made Iona a place for rediscovering inner peace and self-worth as well as a place of prayer and activity for the cause of world peace. Anyone, however, who has heard Lord George MacLeod of Fuinary in full flood at the General Assembly of the Church of Scotland on the subject of nuclear disarmament will have an idea also of the man he looks back to for inspiration for, as Dr John Bannerman of the University of Edinburgh has observed, Columba was a political as well as a spiritual leader and established a relationship between church and state that has affected the story of Scottish Christianity right up to the present day.

Columba was born in Donegal in 522 of the Cenél Conaill royal family and according to a later 'Gaelic life' could have been king, but chose instead chastity, wisdom and that journeying both physically and spiritually that was summed up for the Celtic church in the word 'pilgrimage'. In Ireland he founded a whole family of monasteries that soon overshadowed the Roman-type church established by Patrick. Columba came to Scotland after a savage civil war for which he seems to have felt particularly guilty. It would be all wrong, however, to imagine him coming to Iona to hide or lick his wounds because he continues to be deeply involved both with his monks and with politics in Ireland and began what could only be described as a major new career of influence in first the kingdom of the Scots and then that of the Picts. In Dalriada, he supported Aidán by personally crowning him king of Dalriada, beginning a close political partnership which would ensure not only that

Iona was the mother of a whole family of Scottish foundations but also the place of advice for kings – and their final resting-place. Stories abound of his journey to make an accommodation with King Bridei or Brude of the Picts. This took place at Inverness and centred on a confrontation between Columba and the king's magus or Druid, which of course Columba won with all sorts of displays of wisdom and power! There's even a story about his saving a servant at the crossing of the River Ness from 'a monster' – and so began the long saga of the Loch Ness monster. The engagement with the Picts, however, was real enough and at least in his successors Columba was to bring them Christianity.

Modern excavation at Iona hasn't just revealed the wonderful hundred or so Celtic crosses that go right back to his day and are a story in stone of Christian Celtic communication but has also verified much of the accuracy of the main facts in Adomnán's *Life of Columba*. Once you make allowance for the literary form used by Adomnán, the ninth abbot, the picture emerges of the major cluster of buildings, the agriculture, the writing and decoration of manuscripts and the prayer life. We now know that Iona had scholarship and culture going right back to Columba and the *Book of Kells* itself derives directly from his influence.

## 11   Columba not the only one!

So much is written and spoken about Columba coming from
Ireland to Scotland that it's only too easy to forget the many
others who made the same journey and were revered in their
time. There was a remarkable vitality in the 'journeying' for
Christ which is synonymous with religious life, leaving the
loved and familiar and going with and for God into the
unknown. The Norse in later years were to find the bells and
croziers of Celtic monks in Iceland and Brendan is reputed to
have reached America. A bit nearer home, St Brendan is said by
Adomnán to have visited Columba on Iona from Clonfert in
Connaught. He may well too have founded the monastery on
the Garvelloch Islands in the Firth of Lorne, a place so isolated
that the little beehive cells there are still in fairly good shape.
Bridget, abbess of Kildare, may not have visited Scotland
herself to found Abernethy but it certainly goes back a long way
to her monastery as its mother. Comgall founded the monastery
of Bangor in Belfast, visited Columba and established at least
one monastery in Tiree. Moluag (Lugaidh) has been variously
described as Columba's fierce rival or best colleague with an
exciting story of the two of them racing in coracles to reach
Lismore first. Be that as it may, Lismore was Moluag's base and
an ideal one for his missionary work: probably for that reason it
was chosen as the cathedral of Argyll in the twelfth century.

The most famous saint of all was Kentigern but he's the one
we have the fewest hard facts about, despite the vast number of
dedications to him throughout Scotland and Glasgow's pride in
him. Wells, fairs and chapels are dedicated to him either in his
proper name or his nickname 'Mungo'. Mungo is Brythonic
rather than Gaelic and so would probably have been used in
Strathclyde. The problem is that Jocelyn, bishop of Glasgow
some six centuries later, commissioned a monk, Jocelyn of
Furness, to write 'a good life' of the founder. Professor Kenneth
Jackson describes the result as making Kentigern 'the cuckoo in

the nest' among the Celtic saints for he may be an amalgam of various saints and have doubtful links with leading Celtic figures such as Columba, Serf and David of Wales. The traditional biography has him born at Culross with Enoch as his unmarried mother; then in Glasgow founding a monastery; then in Cumbria and Wales, and lastly to Hoddom in Dumfriesshire and back to Glasgow and Strathclyde. The famous ring and salmon story on Glasgow's coat of arms is a common folk tale, so also is the robin story. What we do know is that he certainly founded the monastery at Hoddom and that Glasgow Cathedral probably derived from the important monastery of Govan, which was part of the legacy of his influence and inspiration. He has a valued place as a Briton in a Celtic monastic tradition that made Scotland Christian by the sheer impact of its presence. It has echoes of the theology of presence in the modern Christian church: the idea that Christians by being united to Christ need only be 'present' to allow Christ to be present and effective through them. They don't need to be always talking about their faith to witness to it.

Glasgow Cathedral (by permission of the Royal Commission on the Ancient and Historical Monuments of Scotland)

## 12  Aidán and Lindisfarne: west goes east

The significance of Iona for the story of the Christian church in Scotland is underlined when west meets east. The heathen Angles had pushed up from England to overwhelm the Christian Britons. Aidán, king of Dalriada, alarmed at their growing power, invaded Northumbria in 603 but was defeated at Degsastán by Aethelfrith. Edwin defeated Aethelfrith in turn and succeeded him as king of Northumbria; and at a later stage he became a Christian. This opened the door for Augustine's missionaries to come north to have mass baptisms at York – until disaster struck again for Christianity in the whole area from York to Edinburgh with the death of Edwin. All seemed lost but help came in a roundabout way. Aethelfrith's sons, Oswald and Oswiu, had been driven by Edwin into exile in Dalriada where they became Christians at Iona. When Oswald came to power in Northumbria, he sent to Iona for a missionary. The first to go was a disaster and had to be recalled. When he reported to the assembled community of Iona his total failure to make headway, the young Aidán (no relation of the king of Dalriada) spoke up: 'It seems to me brother that you were too hard on your ignorant listeners and should first have given them the milk of milder instruction.' With this softly, softly approach, Aidán set off in 635 and was dramatically successful, establishing the great monastery of Lindisfarne in the process.

From Lindisfarne many monasteries were established, including Melrose and Coldingham in south-east Scotland. Like Lindisfarne, they were modelled on the pattern of Iona. Lindisfarne particularly developed the artistic work and learning that marked Iona. Most famous of all is a whole series of small, carefully decorated stones with Latin inscriptions. The most striking example shows a combination of Celtic and continental influence. Then again there was the manuscript tradition that is evidenced so clearly by the still surviving

Lindisfarne gospels. Aidán's story is carefully told by Bede. He was a mild, even humble, person whose remarkable devotion to the Christian ideals of his church allowed him to speak out boldly. The story goes that he silenced a king of the Angles who remonstrated with him when he gave a beggar the horse that the king had just given him: 'Surely this son of a mare is not dearer to you than that son of God?' Echoes then of Christ: 'whatever you do to the least of my brothers, that you do unto me'. Bede recalls too that Aidán walked whenever he could, stopping to talk to everyone no matter who they were. There's perhaps a lesson there for the modern priest and minister with their cars!

In more general terms, Lindisfarne and Aidán bring the days of a Scottish church and nation that much closer. East and west have met and joined hands. Stormy times and relationships lie ahead but progress is now inevitable.

Iona Abbey (*by permission of J. Pagan*)

## 13 Cuthbert and Melrose: the Iona tradition takes root

Cuthbert came from Anglian not British stock and was born in the Borders, probably at Wrangholm in 634. He was to live through the devastation of the yellow plague which reduced the population by a half and lost the monasteries many of their leaders and monks. He himself barely survived but went on to become renowned as patron saint of Northumbria and honoured there and right across the country to places like Kirkcudbright in the west, spanning both the Celtic monastic tradition and the Roman tradition at the time of the debates that culminated in the Synod of Whitby.

In 651, Cuthbert became a novice at the old Melrose Abbey, a typical Celtic foundation in the low-lying horseshoe of the River Tweed about two miles away from the healthier twelfth-century site visited by the tourists today. He was taught by Boisal, a very famous teacher and preacher who became abbot of Lindisfarne and gave his name to the present villages of St Boswells and Newton-St-Boswells. In the scatter of little dwellings inside the *vallum* (ditch) that marked the monastic enclosure, he deepened his inner life – and just as well in view of what lay ahead. He'd been a lively, agile and quick-witted child but had to go through what seems to have been a form of tuberculosis in the knee before embarking on his missionary wanderings through the countryside. A spell in Ripon followed until controversy about the clash between Roman and Celtic customs forced him back to Melrose. After the Synod of Whitby he accepted the Roman customs, even though he was sad about the saintly Colmán preferring to return to Iona when the changes came in. As prior of Lindisfarne, his was the job of enforcing the changes and this he did enthusiastically before withdrawing to be a hermit, first on St Cuthbert's Isle and then on the much more remote Farne Islands where he erected a cell with such high walls that he could only see the sky and the ocean. Then – lest perhaps we could accuse him of spiritual self-indulgence – the last chapter of his life brought a reluctant return to public life as bishop of Lindisfarne in the new-style organisation of classical diocesan structures. The church in Northumbria had fallen into line with the pattern of church government in the rest of England. Cuthbert was consecrated at York by Archbishop Theodore in the presence of the king – a fitting tribute from the new ways to one of the finest representatives of the old. His last trip was to Carlisle where he established the church which still has his name and a school which lasted up to this century. He died in peace in his old retreat on the Farne Islands.

His story is not just an inspiration in personal spiritual terms but also a significant stage in the Iona tradition taking root in Scotland and learning to adapt to new circumstances.

Melrose Abbey, Roxburghshire (*by permission of the Royal Commission on the Ancient and Historical Monuments of Scotland*)

## 14 Synod of Whitby: change the order of the day!

In the year of Columba's death (597), Augustine was sent by the Pope to bring Christianity to the heathen Anglo-Saxon tribes who had swept through England and into south-eastern Scotland. From his diocesan base in Canterbury, his missionaries – men like Paulinus – gradually came north and met up with the Columban missionaries working south from Lindisfarne. When they met, it became clear that the years of enforced isolation of the Celtic church from the continental church had not led to differences in doctrine. The Celtic church, however, had in organisation become centred on the monastic family – with the abbot calling the shots – and still had customs about the date of Easter and the shape of the clerical tonsure which had been refined over the years in the rest of the church. These differences were in one sense trivial but they were visible and so caused a problem. Matters came to a head when Oswiu, king of the Angles, got so fed up with his wife (from Kent) celebrating Easter at a different time that he called the Synod of Whitby so that both sides could agree on a common policy. Dr John Bannerman of the University of Edinburgh says that the description of the Synod as a watershed in the development of the Scottish church and the elimination of the separate 'Celtic' church in favour of a quite different 'Roman' church is quite inaccurate.

The Synod met in 664 at the nunnery at Whitby. The 'Celtic' view was propounded by the saintly Abbot Colmán: the 'Roman' by Wilfrid, a consummate church politician who doesn't seem to have been liked by anyone (including Bede who was in favour of his view). The debate was remarkable for its quality and for the learned documentation that accompanied it. At the end of the day, Oswiu asked them whether it was true that Peter was given the keys of the kingdom of heaven. Both agreed and so the decision was made in favour of the Roman customs. Colmán and some of the monks of Lindisfarne who couldn't accept the changes halved the relics of Aidán and went off to Iona. Iona didn't fully accept the changes until 716 though the Celtic church in southern Ireland had accepted them by 633. Apart from Colmán's group of monks, the changes were well received in Northumbria. There was a rapid reorganisation of church government in Northumbria along Roman lines. Lindisfarne became the see of a diocese with a bishop in charge and then a bishop of the Picts at Abercorn in Lothian, although this doesn't seem to have lasted very long and some don't agree that calling it a bishopric is an accurate description of what happened. Then about 731, Ninian's Whithorn, having become a monastery in the interval, was re-established as a diocesan see. Just as important was the introduction of the Benedictine rule to monasticism – less fiercely ascetic but more conducive to an ordered religious life. Wearmouth (674) and Jarrow (681) became centres of learning and, with men like Bede, became meeting-points of the English and continental church with the churches of the Picts and Scots. At the end of the day – despite the sad cost in terms of some of the monks' natural and admirable conservatism – the Synod brought about growth and development and enabled the Northumbrian church to build on its heritage with the cross-fertilisation of ideas which alone could secure its future. This in turn was to benefit the growth of the Scottish church.

## 15   Adomnán and Iona: apostle of the written word

Adamnán or Adomnán is best known for his *Life of Columba*
but in many other ways towers over the church of the seventh
century and in his well-deserved reputation for scholarship
embodies the status Iona had achieved. Born in Donegal about
624, he was a kinsman of Columba, and, after scholarly study,
eventually became ninth abbot of Iona. His *Life of Columba* is
vivid in its descriptions of everyday life in the monastery and in
its insight into the character of a man who died some twenty-
seven years before he was born. Then again, however, he wrote
'De locis Sanctis' about the holy places in the East which he
derived from a bishop from Gaul who was spending a winter on
Iona. Despite the second-hand information, the detail in his
account proved later to be remarkably accurate and has often
been confirmed by archaeology.

Traditionally kings of both the Picts and the Scots were
buried at Iona, one of many indicators of how important Iona
had become. Adomnán's status as abbot of Iona is again clear
when he journeys to Wearmouth and Jarrow to meet Abbot
Ceolfrith. In the matter of the controversy as to the date of
Easter between Celtic and Roman customs, Adomnán was a
thoughtful convert to the view that the Roman date was correct.
Here he ran into trouble in Iona and the conflict illustrates how
different the Celtic church monasteries were from the medieval
ones. The community had to be taken into account much more
and the inherent strength of the Columban tradition is made
clear when such a formidable character as Adomnán could not
persuade Iona to change. It was in fact only twelve years after
his death in 704 that the changes were accepted.

Adomnán was influential also within the church in Ireland;
Iona was head of the Columban *parouchia* in Ireland. In 697 he
played a leading part at the Synod of Birr in which Adomnán's
Law Code was passed. This raised the status of women, an
interest said to have dated back to a violent attack on a woman

which he saw when with his mother at an early age and to promises he made to her on that occasion. The 'Lex Innocentium' is not exactly 'Women's Lib' but it did become a charter for women and the death penalty for women was abolished. It originally extended also to clerics and children and was designed to protect them both in peace and in war. Guarantees were established to ensure the law was honoured in Ireland, and in Scotland, among both the Scots and the Picts.

Adomnán's importance for today is perhaps that, though his purpose in his rightly famous *Life of Columba* was to increase the stature of both Columba and the Columban family, he brought real attention to detail to Scottish church history and himself became an inspiration like Columba, his mentor. There's a vivid story of him out at 'the bay on the back of the ocean' at Iona. It was a time of drought, the sky so lifeless that the monks were terrified for the harvest. He went to the place of the relics of Iona (psalters and robe) and thence in solemn procession and prayer to the Colliculus Angelorum, now known as the Fairy Mound. The rains duly came. Columba and his chronicler stand shoulder to shoulder as we look back.

Iona Abbey (*by permission of J. Pagan*)

## 16  Pict and Scot – ascetics together

Right from its monastic origins in Egypt, the Celtic church had a harsh streak of voluntarily accepted bodily penance and forsaking the 'pleasures of this world' which persisted right through from the sixth to the eleventh century. This led to the Gael's closeness to nature and sensitivity to beauty and art. In continental terms, it is true that Irish monks such as Columbanus Christianised Europe by their use of the sacrament of penance and penitential practices, which combined severity with the basic principle that Christ's forgiveness was offered in the church to everyone, no matter what they had done. The role of those now honoured as saints within Celtic monasticism was to inspire by example: the more ascetic they were, the better – and this asceticism attracted the famous and the powerful to go to places like Iona 'on pilgrimage' to end their days there. Many did and their presence there heightened the monastery's place in society. Three of the lesser-known saints of the seventh century have left their mark by their ascetic lives but also by that intangible 'extra element' which is hard to pin down so many centuries later.

Donnán appears in the *Annals of Ulster* and *Tigernach* and is associated with places like Kildonan. Two facts are significant. The first is that the claim he was a Pict and that the late story that Columba curtly refused to be his 'anamchara', his soul friend or confessor, are without real foundation and derive from sources which were setting out to discredit saints like Columba. It does not evidence to tensions between Pict and Scot in the Christian church but it is interesting that later generations wished to suggest such conflict. The second fact is recorded in all the accounts of Donnán, reliable and otherwise. He and some of his community were butchered within the refectory of the monastery. It was perhaps an early Viking raid or an attack by sea pirates – or more realistically the cost of any missionary expansion of Christianity. If so, it was unusual and emphasises how little martyrdom accompanied the Christianisation of Scotland.

Mael-rubha came from Bangor in 671, founded the famous abbey of Applecross in Wester Ross in 673 and died in 722. He's widely commemorated in Loch Maree, Amulree, Keith and Dingwall. He illustrates how pagan customs such as the sacrifice of bulls and putting one's head on a sacred stone to ascertain the future were attached to the saints – and persist even when the saints themselves are forgotten. As late as 1656, certain people were accused at Applecross of 'abominable and heathinishe practizes' on his feast-day and in 1678 Dingwall Presbytery accused others of sacrificing a bull to achieve the cure of the sick. To this day his grave in Applecross is a centre of continuing reverence and superstition alike.

Triduana is a much more shadowy figure who lived and was buried at Restalrig just outside Edinburgh. A typical legend attached itself to her as well as to various other saints – that she plucked her eyes out to avoid the attentions of a prince: be that as it may, people in the fifteenth and sixteenth centuries flocked to Restalrig with eye-troubles 'to mend their e'en'. Such religious ideas died hard in Scotland.

St Triduana's Chapel, Restalrig, Edinburgh

## 17 Nechtan: the Picts make their move

The early eighth century sees Scotland divided between four spheres of influence: the Scots in the west, the Britons of Strathclyde, the Northumbrians in the south and east and the Picts in the east and north. The Battle of Nechtansmere (685) ended the very real possibility that the Northumbrians would unite and rule the whole of Scotland but their intellectual centres continued to flourish. Thus it was that when Nechtan, king of the Picts, became worried soon after he began his rule in 706 about the continuing Celtic traditions of Easter and the clerical tonsure, it was to Northumbria and the great monastery of Wearmouth and Jarrow that he wrote for advice. Bede painstakingly records the long, rather turgid letter sent back by Abbot Ceolfrith, detailing the arguments for the Roman customs that had convinced Adomnán and also replying to the king's request for help in constructing a 'church of stone after the manner of the Romans'. The picture of the court when the letter was received makes it clear that the Picts were a long way from the caricature that still exists of them as a people without culture and learning. The letter was translated, discussed and then accepted enthusiastically, at least by the king, for he issued a royal decree for the whole kingdom establishing the Roman customs. The new church would seem to have been dedicated to Peter and may well have been built at Restennet in Angus, where an ancient tower still stands resembling to some degree the tower at Jarrow. One interesting aspect of this affair is the apparent domination of the church by the king. A later record notes that when the Scots took over Pictland, they 'liberated the church which was in servitude up to that time after the custom and fashion of the Picts'. It may well have been too that a Northumbrian-style bishopric was based at Abernethy from this time but we just don't know.

What is certain is that there was some opposition to the decree from the Columban family of monks. In 717, there is a bald entry in the *Annals of Ulster* saying that the Columban community was expelled by Nechtan. This may well be an exaggeration but at the least it's true that those who refused to accept were removed or, like the followers of Colmán at Lindisfarne, removed themselves and headed back for Iona. The tragedy was that by the time they got to Iona they learned that it had already accepted the Roman date of Easter the year before and so the new ways were now standard for the whole Columban family. There's no evidence of other Roman customs coming into Pictland but, if they did, they would have disappeared very soon. Shortly after this Oengus, son of Fergus, led the Picts in expansionism but overstretched himself when he tried to subdue the Britons as well as the Scots. The Viking raids weakened his people still further, and in 843 Kenneth MacAlpin of Dalriada took over. The Picts soon disappeared from the Scottish scene. Folk memory claims that they were exterminated by the Scots: in fact they just became Scots, accepting the language, the culture and in church terms the Iona hegemony. All we have now is their magnificent symbolic stonework: there the cross joins the ancient wisdom to

remind us that the Picts must have made significant contributions to the evolution of the Scottish Christianity that we know today.

Pictish symbol stone, Aberlemno, Angus (*by permission of the Royal Commission on the Ancient and Historical Monuments of Scotland*)

## 18 'The chief relic of the Western world'

In 1007, the *Annals of Ulster* described the *Book of Kells* as the 'chief relic of the Western world'. Although named after the famous Irish Columban monastery where it eventually reposed, scholars are pretty well now agreed that it was begun about 800 in Iona and perhaps finished there also. We can also say that Conachtach, abbot of Iona, who was described as an eminent scribe, may well have been the inspiration of its overall plan and have seen it well on the way before he died in 802. The sort of evidence that has turned this view from wishful thinking to hard fact is multiform. The great wheeled stone crosses of St Martin and St John on Iona show representations of the Virgin and Child surrounded by angels that are only found elsewhere in a page of the *Book of Kells*. Other parallels abound, as on the reliquary from Monymusk which is in the form of a house-shrine made of wood and is almost certainly the 'Breccbennach' of Columba.

The first importance of the *Book of Kells* for the ongoing story of the Christian religion in Scotland is that it reminds us that, as Scotland enters a period of three centuries when we know very little about what was happening in the country far less the church, Iona stands out as having become one of the most important centres of scholarship in Britain. The Dark Ages were a hard brutish time but their most extraordinary characteristic was the pervasiveness and persistence of the Christian faith right through this time when it had no outside source of revitalisation and had to draw deep on the resources of quieter times. The Irish Annals are our main sources for the period and, though they are full of the burnings, war and slaughter which destroyed so much of our manuscript and artefact heritage, they witness to Christianity being very much at the heart of people's lives. Much of that must be credited to the depth of spiritual life built up in the Columban family of monks who founded monasteries throughout Scotland.

Archaeology is producing more and more evidence (though more and more local digs with proper funding and expertise are needed) of the considerable role that religion played in the lives of people at a time when it had none of the opportunities the church has today.

The second vital significance of the *Book of Kells* is the clear illustration it gives that Scottish and Irish Christianity absorbed a massive amount of the insights of Celtic culture. In other words, we can claim a distinctive, religious, handed-on faith. The most outstanding page is the one which begins the gospel of Matthew and it has been described as the finest piece of calligraphy ever produced – but every page is an individual piece of meditation and composition by the monk scribe. The curvilinear treatment of ornament incorporates fantastic animal figures and spiralling foliage which cannot be fully appreciated until we find out much more about the love of nature and symbolic interpretation that presumably stretches right back to the tribal strongholds such as Traprain Law and beyond, as well as to the Bible as understood from their prayer life. We've lost the ancient music of the harp but we still have enough of the art and poetry to be proud of Scottish Christianity.

The Monymusk reliquary, possibly the Breccbennach of St Columba (*by permission of the National Museum of Antiquities Scotland*)

## 19 Scandinavian raids

The Jorvik exhibition in York – with its thousands of visitors to the reconstructed stronghold of York in Viking times – has rekindled interest in the raids and settlements in the British Isles from pagan Scandinavia which began about 800. Scotland was particularly isolated by the process, explaining in part at least why documentary evidence for the period is so sparse. Contact was maintained, however, with Ireland, despite the Viking-infested seas that now lay between them, and thus contemporary Irish annals continue to report Scottish events at intervals. We are in fact learning more and more all the time about the Scandinavian presence from archaeology and from place-name study. It was quite some time before the Vikings adopted what for them was the new religion of Christianity, but long before that conversion they respected and adopted Christian burial practices. Jarlshof in Shetland is the most completely excavated Norse site in the west. Birsay was a Norse farm built on the site of an early Christian monastery and this gave way for a time to the palace and cathedral of the bishop of Orkney. It was in fact only downgraded with the building in the mid-twelfth century of St Magnus Cathedral in Kirkwall, that immense edifice that must have struck a sense of wonder across all the islands as it towered aloft and provided a centre for the community. The metropolitan centre of the diocese of Orkney and Shetland in the medieval period, however, was still Trondheim in Norway. To this day, the Norse element of these islands is important for an understanding of their character, laws and customs.

The first recorded Viking raid to the British Isles was on Iona in 795, but many were to follow and monasteries suffered in abundance. Many like Iona were sited on vulnerable islands while the precious metals used to decorate their shrines and reliquaries made them attractive targets. Gold and silver objects were easily transported and of high value, and so booty of Celtic church provenance turns up all over Scandinavia. Another Viking raid on Iona is recorded in 802 and then a particularly tragic one in 806 when sixty-eight monks were slaughtered. From 825 comes the famous account of the martyrdom of one of the monks because he refused to tell where on Iona he had buried the shrine of Columba. Basically, the more important the monastery, the more likely the raid. When Dunkeld became the centre of the church after 849, it too suffered on a number of occasions; Coldingham was razed to the ground in 870; Melrose was abandoned.

It was a time of fear and great courage in which Christian faith survived against all the odds. We'll leave the last word to a ninth-century quatrain written in Gaelic by a monk of the Celtic church on the margin of a manuscript, poignantly reflecting on the benefits of a wild night at sea:

> Bitter is the wind tonight.
> It tosses the ocean's white hair.
> Tonight I do not fear the fierce warriors of Norway
> Coursing in the Irish Sea.

St Magnus Cathedral, Kirkwall, Orkney (*by permission of the Royal Commission on the Ancient and Historical Monuments of Scotland*)

## 20  Split in the Columban church

Towards the middle of the ninth century, the Scots took over Pictland. This didn't happen all at once but was eventually total and in this process the critically symbolic moment was the transfer of the relics of St Columba from Iona in 849. The new united kingdom was called *Scotia* in Latin and *Alba* in Gaelic: the new legal centre (*caput*) was Scone. This is what brought pressure for the centre of church administration to move east also. Being inland, too, made these centres just a bit safer from the Norse raids and more easily defended when the worst came to the worst. A second pressure came from the problems of the relationship between the two halves of the Columban family. Communications between Scotland and Ireland were much more difficult and the new Scotia or Alba had a sense of identity as a cohesive whole, distinct from the traditional bonds that had stretched across the Irish Sea.

In church terms, there were two consequences for Iona, both of which were administrative. The decision was made before 807, when Kells was begun as a new Columban foundation in Ireland, that the Irish part of the family would be administered from there, but this wasn't effected until 849 because the permanent take-over of the Pictish kingdom hadn't been completed. When it was, the second consequence for Iona was that Kenneth MacAlpin, king of the Scots, decided the centre in Scotland should be further east, namely at the existing monastery at Dunkeld.

The way the fundamental split in the Columban family took place depended on the fact that the spiritual centre of a family of monks was the place where the relics of the founder rested. Thus it was decided to split Columba's relics. The *Book of Kells* – as it's now known – went to Kells where it stayed from that point on. The fragmentary psalter known as the Battling One (because it was used to achieve victory in battle) also went to Ireland. It's said to have been written by Columba himself and is now preserved in the Royal Irish Academy.

It's significant, however, that the most important relic stayed in Scotland. The shrine of Columba was moved to Dunkeld. Another relic, the Breccbennach of St Columba (speckled, peaked one) – a house-shrine – is still preserved in the Royal Museum of Scotland. When Columba's relics were moved east, his crozier went too and was used in 918 to give victory in the battle between Constantine of the Scots and the Danes.

Despite all the destruction by Scandinavians through the centuries, however, a monastic community survived on Iona. The people and events associated with it, as recorded in the Irish Annals, show it to have remained wholly within the Celtic church mould until it became a Benedictine monastery in 1203. Most of all, for the rest of the Dark Ages, Iona continued to be the burial place of the Scots kings. Donald Ban was the last to be 'carried to Colmekill, the sacred storehouse of his predecessors, the guardian of their bones'.

If the Scot today was asked to name the most spiritually significant centre in his country, invariably the answer would be Iona. That tells its own story.

## 21   Dunkeld and 'the Scottish church' (*Ecclesia Scoticana*)

Until 849, it would be possible to argue that there was no such thing as a 'Scottish church' no matter what name you might like to give it. The church of Columba had extended across national and racial boundaries. Not only were there independent kingdoms but the church was formally linked with Ireland in the west and north, and England in the south. A separate Scottish church only came into being as a result of the movement of Columba's relics from Iona to Dunkeld under Kenneth MacAlpin, for Dunkeld then became the centre of the church in the new united kingdom. A Pictish king list suggests that Dunkeld was an ancient Pictish site and ascribes the monastery there to Constantine who ascended the throne in 789. Later it is recorded to have had an abbot and a bishop, indeed the 'chief bishop' – that is, the one with the greatest status, though not territorial jurisdiction, in the whole of Scotland. Crinan, who married the daughter of Malcolm II and became the father of King Duncan, was abbot of Dunkeld, and the title was held for the last time that we know of by Ethelred, a son of Malcolm III and Margaret. The medieval cathedral had secular canons and a bishop subordinate to the see of St Andrews. The edict for the despoiling of the building at the time of the Reformation makes it clear how the last elements linking back to Columba were destroyed: particularly tragic would seem to have been the loss of Bishop Lauder's great reredos which depicted the twenty-four miracles normally ascribed to St Columba.

The question that has to be faced and explored about this period is whether people from 849 onwards had acquired the concept of a 'Scottish church', that is the *Ecclesia Scoticana*. In later ages this phrase was so associated with ideas of Scottish independence from the English that it is used in political and religious arguments with the Pope, and with the English kings when Scotland with Wallace and Bruce was fighting for its life against absorption by England. It must have taken time for people to have started using it but in the Chronicle of the Kings of Scotland, King Giric (878-889) is said to have been 'the first to give liberty to *Ecclesia Scoticana*, which was in servitude up to that time according to the custom and fashion of the Picts'. Arguments rage as to how much or how little this meant at the time. Was it a proclamation of the independence of the church from the close links with state that had existed since Columba and which in the absence of strong church figures meant that kings tended to bring about changes in the church and not vice versa? Or rather does it foreshadow the agreement of 909 between Constantine II and Bishop Cellach at the Hill of Credulitas (faith in the gospel) near Scone where they 'pledged themselves that the laws and disciplines of the faith, and the rights of the Churches and the gospels should be preserved in conformity with [the customs of] Scots'. It is clear then that Dunkeld represents the beginnings of the concept of the Scottish church. The pattern was that ordinary people walked to the nearest monastic church and the monasteries responded by a whole network of little wooden and stone chapels served by monks journeying there to offer mass. Little survives, but work done by Professor John MacQueen of the School of Scottish Studies is by careful study of place names opening up windows into the developing pattern of the Scottish church. With peace and stability the authority of the bishop became eventually a practical reality within this pattern.

## 22  St Andrews emerges from Kilrimont

Anyone at all interested in the story of the Christian church in Scotland knows how central St Andrews is. Not so well known is the name of Kilrimont but that was in fact the name of the monastery that later became known as St Andrews. It's hard to separate legend from fact, but by 747 there was certainly a monastery there and one clearly in the Columban family; Tuathalán, abbot of Kilrimont, is recorded as having died that year. By the twelfth century it was known as St Andrews. Legends abound as to how this came about with a medieval one leading the popularity stakes with its claim that Regulus sailed from Greece with relics of St Andrew and was shipwrecked at Kilrimont. (Dr Johnson confused the issue by calling the cave and intriguing Pictish-looking tower beside St Andrews Castle – of which we really know nothing – St Rule's or Regulus after a hermit who was supposed to have lived there.) A more matter-of-fact but still legendary explanation is that relics came to Scotland via Hexham and that St Andrew was deliberately adopted as a patron by Angus, a Pictish king of about 730, to counterbalance King Nechtan's adoption of St Peter. According to tradition, there were seven churches within the monastery of Kilrimont and it would probably be true to say that one of these was built and dedicated to St Andrew in the reigns of either Angus, king of the Picts who died in 761, or his namesake who died in 834.

What is certain is that Kilrimont or St Andrews succeeded Dunkeld as the centre of the Scottish church. A central character in this development is King Constantine II (903-943) whose length of reign in those troubled times indicates in itself his power and success. He abdicated in 943 to become abbot of the community there. The monastery benefited from this and he used it as a power-base to meddle in the affairs of his successor, King Malcolm. From then on the monastery continued to develop alongside the resident bishops who were distinguished by the titles 'Episcopus Scottorum' or chief bishop of Scotland. Cellach, based either here or back at Dunkeld, is the name of the one who appears in partnership with King Constantine. From then until the Reformation St Andrews figured in that sort of partnership with the ruling kings and did so as the centre of the church in Scotland. When England began to claim both political and ecclesiastical suzerainty towards the end of the eleventh century, the early dedication to St Andrew was used in appeals to St Peter's and the Pope in Rome. Kings like Alexander I claimed that the bishops of St Andrews were always ordained by the Pope himself and played off York against Canterbury in England. On the other hand, Scotland was far from being isolated from contacts with Rome. The self-same Macbeth, who was so distorted by Shakespeare's play for English chauvinist reasons, was in fact a successful and able king for seventeen years. In 1050, he went to Rome and is recorded as scattering money like seed to the poor. St Andrews then is the centre of comings and goings for the emerging Scottish church and nation. In the end, Scotland persuaded the Pope that it should indeed be independent and by the end of the twelfth century it had acquired the unique position of being the

'special daughter of Rome'. 'For God and St Andrew' was not just a battle slogan against the English but a symbol of the remarkable power of Christianity to become the focus of a nation's identity and pride.

Ruins of St Andrews Cathedral
(*by permission of J. Pagan*)

## 23   Culdees: the men of mystery

The Culdees take us into the mystery of the tenth- and eleventh-century church in Scotland. It's still the Dark Ages, and we're still in the dark about most of what happened and how it was that the Christian faith emerged – despite what seemed to be impossible circumstances – to be central to the life of the emergent Scottish nation. At the centre of that mystery are the Culdees, a new style of monks.

Culdees is an anglicised form of two Gaelic words *Céli* and *Dé*. *Céli* is a secular term for a vassal or client; and *Dé* means God; so Culdees can be rendered as companions or clients of God. They began as a reform movement in Ireland as early as the eighth century, a reversion to the ascetic and intellectual aspirations of the monks of the early sixth century. The order became particularly strong in Scotland, perhaps because there were communities of Culdees at Iona, Dunkeld and St Andrews, the three successive centres of the church in the Dark Ages. Other important Culdee monasteries were Abernethy, Brechin, Muthill, Loch Leven, Monifieth and Monymusk. They believed that the spiritual life in the church was in decline and so promoted the strands of desert spirituality, the ascetic life and scholarship. Above all, they didn't care for lay interference in the life of the church. They were, however, part of the political scene in the pattern laid down by Columba himself.

The tenth and eleventh centuries are the era of the Culdees and although Queen Margaret of Scotland argued with the *Ecclesia Scoticana* about certain matters which she felt were contrary to the custom of the continental church, she had nothing but respect for the Culdees. One of the most telling pictures of her life is of her husband Malcolm Canmore patiently having to interpret for her in her conversations with the Culdees. Many communities survived right into the thirteenth century and at St Andrews for much longer than that. Not all monasteries had been under their influence; some like Deer in Aberdeenshire, for example, were never Culdee. Throughout the twelfth century the surviving monasteries, with the Culdees in the forefront, helped to fill in the temporary but inevitable gaps left by the reorganisation of the church along secular lines and as David I – in a remarkably diplomatic way – brought in the new religious orders with the rules of Benedict and Bernard to promote an orderly life, a place was found for the particular gift of the Culdees by merging them with the Augustinian canons who, like the Culdees, were free to move among the people. It didn't always work and other patterns were used: in Brechin the Culdees became secular canons forming the cathedral chapter; and in St Andrews – since they had refused to be absorbed into the Augustinian order as David had intended – they were still recognisable at the Reformation as canons.

In his life of St Kentigern, written about 1190, Jocelyn uses the name Culdees to designate ideal monks. How to define the ideal monk is arguable but what is clear is that this reforming movement was central to the emergence of the Christian church from the Dark Ages and that much research needs to be done to establish the nature of its true contribution to that process.

Restennet Priory, Angus (*by permission of the Royal Commission on the Ancient and Historical Monuments of Scotland*)

# III  THE MEDIEVAL CHURCH

## 24  The love story of a saint

It's not often that romance blossoms at the heart of a development in the history of the Christian church in Scotland. The story of Margaret, queen of Scotland, is the story of Edinburgh Castle, Queensferry, Dunfermline Abbey and a little cave where she prayed that is hidden beneath a pedestrian precinct in Dunfermline town today. It's most of all, however, a story of the love of Malcolm III of Scotland, Malcolm Canmore, for the young girl whom political circumstance, and maybe bad weather, brought to his court in Dunfermline.

History has been unfair to Malcolm. He was far from being the dumb or even savage character of popular tradition. He'd had to be a forceful character as king of Scotland but had years of culture behind him at the court of Edward the Confessor in England. His first wife was dead and the young Margaret appeared as not only beautiful but a ready-made queen of about twenty, with years of training for the role. She had been born in Hungary where her father, a son of Edmund Ironside, had lived in exile after being sent to Sweden by Cnut, the Danish king of England, with the intention that he and his brother should be murdered. When Margaret arrived in Scotland as a refugee, she was given hospitality by Malcolm, then a tender wooing and finally marriage and a family of sons, who as kings were to shape the future of Scotland.

Margaret was everything we would expect of a royal queen. She loved rich dresses and jewellery but what made her different was that she made herself available to ordinary people with their problems and showed her concern for the poor by feeding and caring for them with her own hands every day. No wonder she came to be recognised as a saint in 1250, quite remarkably soon after her death in 1093! The ferry at Queensferry which survived until the building of the Forth Road Bridge was called after her for she ensured that poor people on pilgrimage to St Andrews could cross there for nothing. Her Christian faith was at the heart of all she did. Her early experience in Hungary was of a newly Christian country gradually changing from paganism and that left her with a missionary instinct for the people of Scotland. Scottish Christianity suffered from being isolated from its roots and was divided between English, Irish and Scandinavian areas of influence. She determined to revive it by renewing its origins in places like Iona as well as by bringing it closer to the international dimension of developed Christianity. As a young queen, she harangued the old bishops to establish church discipline about matters such as the Sabbath and children going to communion too early. It wasn't always popular but it was effective! She began the monastery in Dunfermline and helped with St Andrews; she brought new life and vision to the rather stunted church in Scotland. Vivid memories of her remain – such as her distress at losing her Gospel Book, her description of finding it in a stream as a miracle, and the much greater miracle perhaps of its preservation in the Bodleian Library in Oxford to this day, water marks and all!

## 25  David gives the Pope a geography lesson

Visitors to Holyrood Abbey in Edinburgh have become familiar with a very colourful story about David, one of the sons of Queen Margaret who in succession to one another followed Malcolm on to the Scottish throne. It tells, of course, of David being out hunting in the great park and being saved from certain death by the cross which grew from the antlers of a great stag. Fortunately, the story isn't really spoiled by learning that it was borrowed from an earlier legend and attributed to David or that the relic of the 'true cross' of Christ which David zealously found for the abbey he established was of course one of the thousands which abounded in medieval Europe whose authenticity depended more on pious wishes than historical reality. The point of the story was to record David's carrying his mother's wishes for Scotland into practical realities. He organised and made effective both the international dimension and the Scottish dimension Margaret hoped for in the Scottish church.

It wasn't just a matter of the buildings whose ruins we still wonder at – Dunfermline, Jedburgh, Kelso, and so on. Just as importantly he gave Scotland the proper areas of jurisdiction that had given the Christian church elsewhere a measure of stability. The geography of Scotland was quite different from what we now take for granted. Norway had jurisdiction in the far north and the Western Isles: for them the Norwegian church always appointed a bishop of Orkney and a bishop of the isles. To this David now added or consolidated ten bishoprics in which the bishops had a fixed area of responsibility: they could no longer get away with a roving commission which allowed them to neglect the more difficult bits! St Andrews was confirmed as the leading see with Glasgow second in importance.

With regard to the wider church, David continued to draw enrichment from the English church and the continent, as witness Dunfermline's links with Canterbury. He had, however, to make a stand which was to be important not just for the Scottish church but also for the Scottish nation – and that involved giving the Pope a geography lesson. The Pope of the time took seventh-century Roman geography as his model and so thought of Britain as one country full of Anglo-Saxons: so it seemed right that Canterbury should have oversight of the south and York of the north. David successfully defeated this idea though he failed to get Scotland an archbishop of its own to complete its independence. The Scottish king had a say in appointing Scottish bishops in the usual medieval pattern for rulers but the Pope, rather than an English archbishop, saw to their consecration. This direct link with the Pope guaranteed the prized independence of the Scottish church.

## 26  David gives folk a local kirk

Most of us today in Scotland tend to take the local kirk for granted – and the parish system that goes with it. It wasn't established across the whole of Scotland in its one thousand-odd parishes until the mid-thirteenth century but it was Queen Margaret's son David in the mid-twelfth century who made it possible. It wasn't that he put an ordnance survey type grid over Scotland and decided on the parish structure. Much then was dependent on circumstances and the availablility of landowners' patronage but David's critical contribution was to establish the system of teinds or tithes. Everyone who bred animals, who fished, undertook commerce and so on had now to pay 10 per cent of their profits to the church for the support of a local priest and parish. This provided the final link for the system of local bishops. Although still often advised by the landowners, the bishop appointed parish priests who by reason of the teinds were now independent of the landowners' control. This independence has been valued ever since in the Scottish kirk.

Some of the great abbeys such as Melrose and Holyrood were also parish churches with part of the church set aside for this purpose. Other buildings had to be specially built. The ideal was that a parish should be formed by a day's walk in any direction. The old round towers and wood and wattle buildings of the earlier age were now seen to be inadequate, especially in the light of the influences from England and the continent which David encouraged. From now on the local kirk was at least a powerful symbol of the Christian presence. It tended to dominate the landscape as well as people's lives: but was it only a symbol or mere mythology? Here a lot more work has to be done. In some ways the local church was the welfare state of the day for the poor, the sick and the disabled in a society where local famine was still endemic. How much teaching was done? Parish priests tended not to be well educated and were usually the younger sons of the laird or landowner, able to read and write but with only a little smattering of the gospels for preaching. They were certainly of importance for funerals and there were prominent ceremonies and processions to the burial grounds that are still the most significant way of identifying the location of the old kirks. Marriages were in public, but not necessarily performed even at the porch of the church. We know that the ideal was at least communion at Easter but how much the Sunday mass was attended we simply don't know. What we do know and can say quite safely is that the parish kirk provided a locally responsible priest, whom it would be difficult to ignore, for a people who would never meet the Pope or rarely even their bishop. That local identification is still a challenge for the kirk today.

## 27 The new monks and nuns changing the landscape

The most striking sights a medieval peasant would ever see were the great abbeys which resulted from the vision of Margaret, Edgar, Alexander and, above all, King David I. Teams of masons from England and the continent combined with local labour. There were Benedictines and Cluniac Benedictines, Cistercians in a great line from Rievaulx to Melrose, Newbattle, Kinloss, Coupar Angus and Culross; and Tironensians from Tiron near Chartres. The ruins are impressive enough but we have to imagine them roofed, with statues and great paintings adorning the plaster wherever the eye could stray. The beautifully coloured stained glass added excitement and life and the whole story of the Bible was there in the decoration for everyone to read. The *Book of Kells* shows meditative reverence and scholarship combined. The engineering, as at St Andrews Tower, was daring: there were spectacular collapses but they just started again and got it right. There were two sorts of possible impact: the Cluniac emphasis on brilliance of worship and colour as at Paisley and Crossraguel, contrasting with the awesome austerity of the Cistercian buildings that embodied the simplicity of St Bernard that was so admired by John Calvin himself in a later era.

Nothing succeeds as much as success and nothing is so dangerous: and that is the story of the medieval monasteries. Even the Cistercian abbeys became incredibly wealthy because they were so good at farming that their grain and wool were sold abroad, being shipped out of Berwick, especially to the Low Countries. This helped to add to the splendours of the building of Melrose and Newbattle, while the 'black canons' (Augustinian) at Jedburgh and the 'white canons' (Premonstratensians) at Dryburgh also built their churches out of wool sales.

Again too the personnel of the monasteries and convents had its effect. Some came from poor backgrounds, some from the nobility, but most came from the younger sons and daughters of substantial peasants and burgesses. The discipline of monastery life, however, gave abbots what we'd call today interpersonal organisational skills and these made them the invaluable advisers to bishops and kings alike. This brings power and power can all too often corrupt. When we try also to assess the impact of these monasteries on the local people, we have to contrast the inevitable and catalogued impact of an abbey like Arbroath on the local scene with the fact that in some ways the cloistered life of the abbey, when lived to its ideals, should have little contact with the outside world. The hospitals were mainly for members of the monastery but the great duty of hospitality was always a call to the monks that pushed them to have social significance not just as providers of local employment but as witnesses of Christian caring. History will probably never be able to assess how Christ would have rated the integrity of the Christian message embodied in the symbols but as symbols they certainly had a central impact on medieval society.

## 28 Here come the friars!

That popular welcome made the friars – a still further new style of religious – appear as a threat to John Knox as late as the Reformation. Dominicans and Franciscans were to the towns of Scotland what the Benedictines and Cistercians were to the countryside: they were trained to preach in the language of the people and forbidden to have the cloistered life and wealthy buildings which often separated the older communities from the people and confused their vows of personal poverty. The Scottish climate stopped the friars from being the wanderers they usually were, so when they arrived in the 1230s, the Dominicans and Franciscans settled on the edges of towns such as Berwick, Haddington and Edinburgh in the belief that the parish system didn't reach the town poor. The kings saw the virtue of this despite tensions with the parish clergy who resented them. Poverty was chronic in medieval towns and Scotland's were no exception. Unemployment varied with the seasons and with people's occupations. Sickness was rife. The friars were respected for their work right up to the end of the Middle Ages when defections from their number brought them into disrepute but by the eve of the Reformation they were on the upsurge rather than in decline: new Franciscan friaries were built at nine burghs between 1463 and 1505; there were influential friars at the courts of James IV and James V, like William of Touris who wrote the great poem 'the contemplacioun of Synnaris', the summit of the Poetry of the Passion, for James IV's marriage. Like the Hospitallers of St John who came in David's time, they brought an international flavour. While the Hospitallers opened up an awareness of the Holy Land and led to a steady trickle of Scots distinguishing themselves on the crusades, the friars opened up plain speech on biblical issues for plain folks. Like the Reformers after them, people like Andrew Simpson of Dunning in Perthshire journeyed to listen to the friars' sermons. John Knox – while condemning their Romish ways – still witnesses to how near to the bone and therefore effective were their sermons. He quotes one of them comparing the suffering of purgatory to the suffering a man can experience from a nagging wife. Just a little earlier, the bishop of Dunkeld used them to great effect in his diocese and sought out their services eagerly.

What then of their effectiveness and quality of Christian faith? One of the problems is that the history of the time was written by church people who tell the good things of religious life but gloss over the undoubtedly monstrous cruelty and suffering in society of which we catch only glimpses and which the friars should have attacked more fiercely. Despite the persisting names – Greyfriars and Blackfriars – we don't have great buildings and religious sites to quarry into for clues. All we can say is that there are more good vestiges than bad in the story of the friars.

## 29  Building for God

The Middle Ages were undoubtedly the era when buildings embodied the place Christian folk felt God should have in their community. In an age when other buildings were small and unimportant, the cathedrals must have been overwhelming in their impact. Even today, the way St Magnus Cathedral dominates Kirkwall is breathtaking – what was it like then?

Scotland drew from the mason crafts of England, France and Ireland in the rebuilding of Iona by the Benedictines from 1200 onwards. Irish masons began the work but West Highland craftsmen went on to incorporate all the rich natural symbolism of the Celtic and continental traditions with their use of rich foliage to witness to perfection and the love of nature. The English rebuilt Melrose and the French Jedburgh. Jedburgh and St Andrews stood comparison with the best of Norman tradition and English achievements but the fourteenth-century revival after the poverty of the Wars of Independence sees less ambitious buildings which none the less combine a distinctive Scottish tradition with that of the continent. The Low Countries had a special influence on Rosslyn (Roslin), Crichton and many collegiate churches. Even in spite of economic difficulties, there was rebuilding of outstanding quality at the cathedrals of Glasgow and Dunkeld and at the abbey church of Melrose.

There developed quite a contrast between the simple stone parish churches of the fourteenth century and the great cathedrals (though collegiate status for many parish churches in the fifteenth century changed this) but both seemed to throb with the ordinary lives of ordinary people in addition to their spiritual purpose. The parish churches had two doors, statues and stained glass but no seats or pews or even normally pulpits. Most lasted until the eighteenth century so were substantial edifices. Well-known ones were St Nicholas, Aberdeen; St John's, Perth; Holy Trinity in St Andrews and St Giles in

Edinburgh: all were added to in piecemeal ways over the intervening centuries, with side-altars and aisles dedicated to individual saints. There were sanctuary churches with their special characteristics at Tain, Whitekirk and Torphichen, and pilgrimage churches such as Whithorn, Glasgow and St Andrews, where the design catered for wide passages to allow processions around the centre.

Perhaps the best picture is the great cathedral as a reflection of all medieval life in one building. At one end – behind the rood screen – was the clerical or monastic liturgy: quiet, hidden, mysterious and mystical in its worship and beauty. Then there was the long, open nave throbbing with life. People dropped by to say prayers at the opening to the mystery but also thronged the rest of the cathedral to talk, to have lawyers write up documents and to do business. The poor felt at home in their building: they identified with local saints and were impressed by the great international saints. Above all, it was their public hall and community centre. Life went on there and gave at least a nod to God!

Melrose Abbey, Roxburghshire (*by permission of the Royal Commission on the Ancient and Historical Monuments of Scotland*)

## 30   A Scottish church forming a Scottish nation

The role of the local church in making a nation cohere is one of the fascinating areas of discussion in the history of most Christian nations. The role of the church in medieval Scotland could arguably be compared to the role of the church in Poland today. *Ecclesia Scoticana* is the phrase that sums it up – the Scottish kirk – and Professor Geoffrey Barrow of the University of Edinburgh believes very firmly that one of the most fascinating things about the Reformation in Scotland is the take-over straight from the Middle Ages in the new forum of a Protestant General Assembly of the 'Scottish church' concept and its development in the sixteenth, seventeenth and eighteenth centuries so that 'when the church met, it was the nation in conference'.

The *Ecclesia Scoticana* concept goes right back to David I's successful arguments with the Pope about the Scottish church's independence of York and Canterbury. Although they had no archbishop until 1472, the principal Scottish bishop was the keeper of their privileges and the Pope their guarantor. The year 1192 saw the bold declaration, 'there shall be a Scottish church', and this was the springboard for defending the other proposition that there was a Scottish independent nation. The church was in the forefront from 1296 until 1320 in putting the case for Scottish independence against the claims of Edward I and it was no accident that the famous Declaration of Arbroath to Pope John in 1320 was the work of a churchman. Baldred Bisset studied on the continent but in the 1290s and 1300s, he lobbied the Pope with a propaganda campaign for Scottish independence.

All in all, of course, the rapport between the Scottish church and the kings was quite remarkable. Both benefited. Monasteries and parish kirks alike were established by royal patronage. They benefited financially and the king benefited because the spiritual power in each area was appreciative of that patronage and so would tend to defend his interests. This led to the confrontation of the Scots bishops with the claims of England. Robert Wishart was bishop of Glasgow from the 1270s until 1316 and a stout friend of Robert Bruce, neatly producing the robes for his enthronement at the appropriate moment, as if by magic! He was gaoled in Winchester for his loyalty. As with the rest of Scottish life, there were mixed attitudes to Bruce in the church but on the actual independence issue, the Scottish church was totally consistent. William Fraser and William Lamberton of St Andrews were strong supporters of William Wallace and Balliol but at the end of the day Lamberton made it clear that in all the rivalries 'what mattered was what was best for Scotland', and so he supported the abandoning of Balliol in favour of Bruce. 'Church and Nation' in the kirk today may well echo still this sort of decision-making by the Christian church.

Arbroath Abbey, Angus (*by permission of the Royal Commission on the Ancient and Historical Monuments of Scotland*)

## 31 Hard times mean new types of kirk

In the late Middle Ages, the nobility didn't have money to build big abbeys. What they did was to gather together a group of priests or monks – a college, it was called – for a quite specific purpose. In an era which feared the power of the devil and was concerned for the after-life, many foundations of this sort resulted from kings or nobles wanting provision to be made for masses to be offered for their souls after they died, to make up for the sins they committed in life. These the later Protestant Reformers were of course to see as particularly useless. Other colleges of perhaps five to twelve priests were gathered to look after a parish and some were meant to found schools. Professor Ian Cowan of the University of Glasgow is rather sceptical about how much education resulted, but Professor Geoffrey Barrow of the University of Edinburgh prefers to stress the fact that these colleges, as the name implies, were to be the seedbed on which the universities were founded and in their own right mark an important stage in the Scottish tradition of education for all.

In any case, what is clear here for our developing history of the Christian church in Scotland is that these colleges of priests gave us what are known as collegiate churches. Rosslyn, Seton, Restalrig, Trinity, Dunbar, Lincluden (Dumfries) are all names to conjure with in this regard. Many undoubtedly gave their communities real benefit: some we have no way of knowing about but we have knowledge of others. Of these latter, St Giles in Edinburgh and Holy Rude in Stirling are well catalogued for the good they did for the community. Many kirks still continue the tradition of medieval collegiate churches: it's a fascinating area of research to find out the prehistories of the local kirks in our own areas. Each has a story all of its own. Even the names of the altars give a clue to the society around them: St Obert was the patron of the baxters, St Crispin of the skinners, and so on. To take a random example:

not many people know that Waverley Station in Edinburgh is built on the site of Trinity College collegiate church which was founded by Mary of Gueldres in 1460 after the death of her husband, James II. There was an outcry when it was decided to demolish it to make way for the station. A compromise was reached in which the building would be taken down stone by stone and the stones numbered so that it could be built elsewhere. The irony was that there was so much argument about where to build it that the numbering had worn off the stones by the time an agreement could be reached. Only a few stones to the south of Waverley mark this sad episode. There is talk of reconstructing part of it at Jeffrey Street but the episode highlights how the legacy of the past has to be thought about carefully and its enduring lessons preserved.

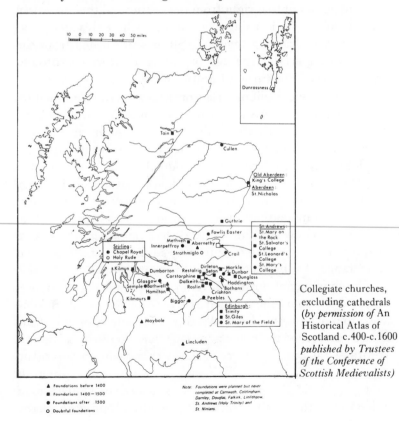

Collegiate churches, excluding cathedrals (*by permission of* An Historical Atlas of Scotland c.400-c.1600 *published by Trustees of the Conference of Scottish Medievalists*)

▲ Foundations before 1400
■ Foundations 1400 – 1500
● Foundations after 1500
○ Doubtful foundations

*Note: Foundations were planned but never completed at Carnwath, Coldingham, Darnley, Douglas, Falkirk, Linlithgow, St. Andrews (Holy Trinity) and St. Ninians.*

## 32  Church and university

The university students of today would hardly regard themselves as church students but that is how it all started. Bishop Henry Wardlaw of St Andrews decided on a Scottish university to improve the education of the clergy and the people as a whole. Helped by civil war in France, he was able to achieve a brain drain in reverse to establish what we would now see as a tiny college. Students were numbered in dozens or scores at most and there would only be a dozen or so teachers but Professor Geoffrey Barrow of the University of Edinburgh loves to point out that right from the beginning, the university was a collective learning community where teachers and students kept learning together. Studies proceeded from the seven liberal arts at the age of twelve or thirteen through mathematics, literature (Latin) and philosophy (science, astronomy, logic) right up to law or theology as the culmination of development. It was an all-male community with little time for leisure and with the authorities inveighing against the playing of football. These habits died hard: a dozen years after the Reformation, Glasgow town council grudgingly conceded that teachers at its university might marry but they had to keep their wives off campus! Despite the high profile of theology which the modern university would find unacceptable, Professor Barrow sees the early days as a reminder of the value of the Scottish tradition of university study being fairly general in its range of subjects covered.

The church continued to develop a quite remarkable growth of university provision for such a small country. James I in 1424 tried to move St Andrews to Perth to keep an eye on it but the church preserved its independence. James Kennedy advanced it with St Salvator's College whose tower and church can still be seen in North Street. William Turnbull, the bishop of Glasgow, decided to catch up and established the University of Glasgow in the High Street, close to the Dominican friars.

Then Bishop William Elphinstone of Aberdeen – with the king's help – established King's College (originally the college of St Mary in the Nativity) in Old Aberdeen, thus making three universities in Scotland by the end of the fifteenth century.

The universities meant that Scotland was able to shine in Europe as well as raise standards of education at home. The poor were able to advance. They had a harder time, however, and often acted as servants to the richer students and had to eke out the grain they brought until they could go back home on 'Meal Day' to get more. The rich students often paid the graduation fees to the teachers for everyone: and a college for poor students (St Leonard's) was established at St Andrews. The lad o' pairts could shine in the debates and become skilled in logic as a tool for all the other disciplines. The best of them went on to a second degree on the continent, usually at Louvain, Cologne or Paris. One story worth following up is that of John Mair who was taught at the grammar school in Haddington, shone at the University of Paris and was persuaded by the poet Gavin Douglas to bring his formidable reputation to the University of

Glasgow. He lived long enough to be finally saddened by the coming of Luther's ideas but was clearly still very much in touch at the end as at the beginning of his long life of study. A Scot to be proud of.

Arms of James IV and Margaret Tudor, King's College, Aberdeen (*by permission of the Royal Commission on the Ancient and Historical Monuments of Scotland*)

## 33   Of saints and sinners

In an age when we tend to consider ourselves as an odd mixture of saint and sinner, it's hard to imagine the medieval attitude which encouraged people to see themselves as sinners and look back to the saints of the past to help them improve. Dr John Durkan of the University of Glasgow likes to joke about the number of Celtic saints being so great that 'saint' became just another word for 'Mister'. Only a few are now well known but a fascinating area of local research is to be found in the place names of Scotland for a vast number of these go back to the old Celtic saints. Many of them disappeared in the twelfth and thirteenth centuries when the links with the continent brought in dedications to the internationally known saints, sometimes in a single dedication and sometimes in a joint dedication (St Mirrin is St James and St Mirrin). The other side of this is that Scots going abroad have marked their path by dedications of little chapels to saints like St Ninian, St Columba and St Mungo (even though nothing much is known about him). At home, internationally known saints tended to be introduced for a whole range of different reasons. The Cistercian monks brought devotion to Mary (always pictured with the child Jesus) as can be seen at Melrose still. By the twelfth century, if not before, sailors brought St Nicholas to St Andrews, Aberdeen and the parish church at Renfrew. St Roch came in after the plague: there's a well-documented case as late as the early sixteenth century of a chapel being founded to ward off further plagues. St Catherine of Alexandria came in to encourage learning. St Sebastian (and his arrow-pierced body) was invoked to help cope with suffering – and there was plenty of that around; craft guilds brought their own saints, like St Eloi of the metal-workers (or hammermen). It all sounds very esoteric now but it's worth noting that the medieval Scot was very practical about his idea of the heaven he looked forward to. A great lake of ale for all eternity wouldn't be out of place as a description.

In more serious vein, many medieval Scots – and not just St Margaret – became universally known and respected for their sanctity. This took different forms of course. The story is told of the priest Thomas, who, when the Edinburgh garrison fled before the advancing English, stood alone on the ramparts and solemnly excommunicated the king and his army. That took courage of a special kind. Adam of Dryburgh went to the local abbey, made good, studied on the continent and became revered in a Carthusian monastery in Somerset. And then there was John of Duns, a poor boy from a poor family, who by the early fourteenth century was revered as one of the great philosophers of Europe and the most pre-eminent theologian of the value of love. The fact that his philosophy went out of fashion led to his name 'Duns Scotus' being abused as 'dunce'. He was in fact the 'subtle doctor' – of whom Scotland today can be proud.

## 34 The monks revive – but too late!

The fifteenth century was a time of attempted reform in the Christian church. Council after council met to try to achieve improvements worldwide but failed miserably. The opening speeches of the Fifth Lateran Council at the beginning of the sixteenth century were such that they might well have made the Reformation split unnecessary, but they came to nothing – or not enough.

The Franciscans and Dominicans in Scotland did take up the reform movement, however, and it caused a fair bit of commotion. Dominicans especially were often to the fore, as early Protestant converts or as the shock-troops of Catholic attempts to reform the church from within. John Adamson, OP, had to face riots because of his attempts to bring in Protestant-style reforms in Aberdeen in 1543: but in 1559 in Edinburgh, John Black, OP, said mass at Holyrood while, half a mile away, John Knox preached as the first Protestant minister of St Giles.

More significant, perhaps, was the Cistercian reform in abbeys like Kinloss, which lies just outside Elgin. Bishop Robert Reid of Orkney, who was to leave a major endowment to what would later become the University of Edinburgh, brought Giovanni Ferrerio from Paris to teach. After a spell at the court of James V, he arrived in Elgin bringing biblical studies and the first signs of humanist and Renaissance learning to the monastery. There was a revival of the ancient craft of the scribes for its meditative value, even though their work in the printing age was in much less demand. Spiritual and intellectual life revived with the newly established University of Aberdeen as the focus. When Lutheranism arrived through the northern seaports, there was positive debate and thoughtful resistance on such points as the loss in the Reformers of reverence for the reserved sacrament. There are examples of sacrament houses being built to replace the hanging pyxes for the same reason. All of this meant that, after the Scottish Reformation, there was much resistance in the north-east and Protestantism north of the Tay has a different, less destructive tone than that of central Scotland. Forres, Elgin and Lossiemouth were examples of both edifying religious life and the new knowledge, evidenced by the use of Melanchthon's Grammar in tandem with the traditional faith.

Other reforms should not be forgotten: again too little, too late, from the point of view of those who wished continuity with the past. John Winram (who became a Protestant Reformer later) is on record in his days as subprior at St Andrews for a visitation to Pittenween in 1554. He insisted that they should get up at six for matins in the summer and seven in the winter; that they should add lauds to their daily prayer on the grounds that the praise and solemn music would be appreciated by the people on solemn feasts; and that no boys should be allowed in the dormitories at night – a curious ruling which could have reflected corrupt sexual practices or a rather over enthusiastic way of ensuring a supply of novices by attracting them early to religion. The answers to this and other aspects of the pre-Reformation reforms still have to be discovered.

Monks' Tower, Perth, demolished in 1806 (*by permission of the Royal Commission on the Ancient and Historical Monuments of Scotland*)

## 35 Popular religion and popular grievances

The medieval practice of the Christian religion in Scotland does not seem to have built up the same pressure of resentment that made the Reformation so popular in other areas of Europe. There were pardoners selling indulgences to all intents and purposes, but not to the same corrupt extent as those who annoyed Luther. There was a fear of these things, which had worried Luther, but in Scotland in the late Middle Ages there still seems to have been a balance with a cheerful side in the plays and processions of the sacrament. Professor Geoffrey Barrow of the University of Edinburgh observes that the corrective role of the clergy with the discipline of church courts made for patches of local unpopularity. Professsor Ian Cowan of the University of Glasgow notes that the religious houses were mostly left alone at the Reformation, except when the mob was directly induced to attack them or where there was local bad blood as between Lindores and Dundee. He is on record too attacking the popular misconception that people weren't going to church. Masses went on all day, every day, and people popped in as it suited them. The fact that commercial stalls were set up around the church and sports organised there both point to people using the church building.

There are issues to be balanced. On the one hand, the church started plays and pageants, as at Corpus Christi, to teach people the truths of faith: these truths were illustrated vividly on the church walls and windows for all to see; but on the other hand preaching was neglected, except by the friars, and the Bible tended to be feared in its new printed translations. Saints lay at the heart of ordinary everyday life but (as a result) also fell prey to resentments, whether religious or economic. In 1558 in Edinburgh, the statue of St Giles was stolen: the council borrowed a small one for the annual procession celebrating the burgh's patron saint on the first day of September but the mob attacked it. Professor Cowan sees this as evidence of a quarrel between the church and town council as to who should pay for a new statue; Dr Michael Lynch of the University of Edinburgh sees it as the Protestant minority declaring themselves with a public gesture.

Perhaps the biggest areas of grievance were twofold. The Middle Ages saw evil as a force which had to be combated by poverty: and yet the king's patronage and the successful development of both farming and piety had brought great wealth to the religious communities. They may or may not have lived poor lives as individuals but they lived in massive buildings surrounded by riches, power and privilege. When people had to pay rents, tithes and other duties, resentment built up.

Secondly, the parish system had fallen into neglect. By the time of the Reformation, over four-fifths of the parish teinds had revenues diverted to support other communities, whether religious houses, universities or collegiate churches. The parish priests themselves were mostly absent or 'were institutions'

themselves and the vicars or curates appointed in their stead for the weekly parish work were ill paid, ill educated and ill trained. There was also indiscipline and sexual immorality but plain old-fashioned neglect was the main cause of popular grievance.

Rosslyn Chapel, Midlothian
(*by permission of the Royal Commission on the Ancient and Historical Monuments of Scotland*)

# IV THE SIXTEENTH AND SEVENTEENTH CENTURIES

## 36 Catholic cult in late medieval towns

What is remarkable about Catholic cult and worship in late medieval towns is that, far from being remote from real life, it was totally responsive to and shaped by the changes in town life which resulted from the craft guilds being given incorporated status in the burghs. Aberdeen Burgh Records in the first half of the sixteenth century catalogue the precedence disputes of the various guilds for the Candlemas and Corpus Christi processions, pride of place being of course as near as possible to the blessed sacrament. Their banners proclaimed their patron saints:

> Skynnaris Sanct Stewin and his tormetouris.
> The tailyeouris the Coronation of Our Lady.
> Baxtaris Sanct Georg.
> Wrichtis messonis sclateris and cuparis The Resurrectioun.
> The smithis and hemmirmen The Barmen of the Croce.

This sort of piety was very much in line with what was happening on the continent. Thus the Edinburgh Burgh Records (December, 1518) note the devotion to the holy blood which came straight from Bruges:

> My Lord Provost, president, baillies, counsall and community hes gevin the Holy blude Ile to the fraternity of the merchant and gild brethie of this burgh, and that to be patronis thairof, and the octaves of Corpus Christi to be their procuratioun dayes.

Because of this piety that so clearly was integrated with people's real perceived needs, the sixteenth century can be described as the most medieval of all – and the Catholic cult was fresh, alive and responding to needs. The Baxter Book of St Andrews (28 October 1558) noted that John Miller 'has pait his pund of wax to ye alter of Sant Cobert'. Routine, yes, but clearly part of life. The Protestant James Baron, Edinburgh Dean of Guild, 1555-1556, carefully noted the expenses of the celebration of Christmas, new glass in the windows, singing of the Passion, 'keiping of the Sepulcur' at Easter and looking after 'Sanct Gelis arme'.

The last component of the new wave of Catholic piety came in the form of the cult of the Passion of Christ. Here the contributors were often Observant Franciscans and the high point of the 'Poetry of the Passion' came in the work written by the friar William of Touris in 1499 and dedicated to James IV. It was called the 'Contemplacioun of Synnaris' and took the form of a devotion of seven poems arranged to follow the days of the week. The theme for Friday was remembrance of the Passion of Christ and the compassion of Mary. The 'Contemplacioun' was rearranged by the editor of the famous Bannatyne Manuscript in 1568 and it got past a censorship committee of the new Protestant kirk! The same sort of religious

devotion is shown pictorially in the only craft banner to have survived to the present day. It's called the 'Fetternear Banner' and in addition to the rosary, shows the instruments of the Passion and the devotion to the holy blood that's referred to in a whole series of altars in Scotland. Although some forms of Catholic piety – the rosary, devotions addressed to the saints and the virgin Mary – were cast aside at the Reformation, Protestant writers could and did use other forms, and especially the Passion.

The Fetternear Banner (*from* Essays on the Scottish Reformation 1513-1625 *published by Burns*).

## 37 Luther makes his mark – or does he?

The old version of the story of the Scottish Reformation was that it began with the Lollards of Kyle in 1499, continued with the Lutheran Reformers and, in a developing process, culminated in 1560. In fact, the Lollards of Kyle showed the anticlericalism of the English Lollards but had little influence outwith this area, even though there are suggestions that Aberdeen college in 1506 was designed to combat its dangers. If so, it was a needless fear. On the continent, Luther began the Reformation in 1517 but in Scotland the 1520s saw a major importation of fresh devotions of honour to the saints from trading links with the Netherlands. Trade, too, however, brought Lutheran books to Scotland from the Baltic ports and so successive Acts of Parliament forbade such imports in 1525 and 1535. As with any banned books, however, they did have a very real influence among some of the educated lairds: after all, Protestantism is a religion of the book in the first instance. That influence as yet was still very much on the fringes of Scottish life.

Patrick Hamilton came from one of Scotland's leading families and met Luther in Wittenberg. When he returned to the University of St Andrews, his unbridled enthusiasm created its own backlash and this led to his execution, even though no one really seems to have wanted this to happen. His death, however, had little influence, except to discourage those who wished to dally with 'heretical ideas'. There were few martyrs; some found refuge on the continent and many were to find a warm welcome in Edward VI's England. James V had been more severe with Protestantism after his marriage to Mary of Guise in 1538 but his death in 1542 introduced a situation of uncertainty in which the Protestants saw their opportunity: the English connection gave them hope and yet also meant that they risked rejection by those who hated the English more than the French.

In this situation, George Wishart was to make a great impact on the Protestant cause by his death at the guilt-ridden and hesitant hands of Cardinal Beaton. His preaching had its roots in Luther and Zwingli and had some success in Montrose, Dundee and Ayrshire, sowing seeds that were to come to fruition in later years when the Reformation proper arrived. It was his Christ-like kindness to plague victims in Dundee, however, rather than his denunciation of idols that brought him most popularity. His downfall came when he met major opposition from the landowners in Lothian and Haddington. Everyone in Haddington seemed to have preferred a 'clap play' to his sermon and eventually all but three of his supporters deserted him. He may or may not have been an English spy: fundamentally he fell victim to the church making an example of him and hoping people would soon forget. In the short term the people did, especially when the murder of Cardinal Beaton was as equally repulsive to them as Wishart's own death. The Reformers left for the galleys but the bad taste left in the mouth was to be a major factor when the cause of the Protestant Reformers became politically more acceptable. The Lutheran reform had failed in Scotland and Zwingli and Calvin were to shape the final reform in its place.

## 38 The condition of the church

One of the great myths in the history of the Scottish
Reformation is that the established church (what we would now
call the Roman Catholic church) was in a state of terminal
decay. There were areas of neglect, such as the poor status of
the parish clergy and there was an ever-increasing burden on
the lairds and landed people in what was a century of rising
inflation. This bred resentment of the church but on the other
side of the question were a whole number of factors reviving
church life. Bishop Elphinstone of Aberdeen had led a whole
movement to restore the Scottish saints and this identification
factor was popular. Provincial Councils in 1549, 1552 and 1559
were frank about the immorality of the clergy and their failure
to be pastoral, and were scathing about financial exactions. In
the statutes of the forties and fifties, bishops were ordered to
visit everyone at least every two years; priests were instructed to
build reverence for the sacraments and eliminate superstitious
practices, such as breaking hosts on the fields. The ordinary
parish priests or chaplains were, however, popular, meeting
real needs by saying masses for loved ones who had died: they
were a bridge to them as well as to God. Their duties were
closely supervised by lay patrons who were often ordinary folk.
St Giles in Edinburgh was not unusual in having forty-five
altars, each with a chaplain who followed duties laid down by
the patron. Masses went on from five in the morning until late at
night and the chaplains would often be boarded out with
members of the guild. In a very real sense, the church and the
people were becoming much closer.

Much of this was due to the Cistercian reforms at the top end
of society and the reforming friars at the bottom end. Within
the towns much too was tied in with the growth of the craft
guilds from 1500 onwards, for in this sphere secular position
and religious guarantees went hand in hand. Each guild
(masons, bakers, hammermen, and so on) had their own saints

and they had their own place in the great pageants, processions and plays which gave scope both for religious enthusiasm and practical Christian teaching. Catholic popular religion was more popular than ever before.

And what about sexual morality? Protestant historians of the nineteenth century took great glee in cataloguing the bastards of the clergy. Two things have to give us pause before we hold up our hands in horror and say 'That's what went wrong'. First, the fact that most of the clergy seemed to have been very faithful to what could well be described as proper common-law wives. The bishop of Aberdeen lived happily with Marjory Urquhart for thirty years; Cardinal Beaton with Marion Ogilvie for twenty years. Linked with this is the second fact that the Council of Trent was expected by many to recognise again that marriage was an option for priests. The Protestant Reformers, however, had adopted that position so the Council, as with their use of the vernacular in place of Latin, did the opposite. To balance the picture too we should note that Bishop Alexander Gordon of Galloway, who turned Protestant in 1560, made no bones to the Perth kirk session about his long-standing extra-marital relationship or his children.

Sexual practices and financial matters apart, there was much about the pre-Reformation church in Scotland that was healthy and so the success of the Reformation in making Scotland Protestant was far from being a foregone conclusion.

## 39   George Wishart – Protestant 'saint'

George Wishart stands out in the Reformation struggle as perhaps the finest bridge person as Roman Catholics and Protestants today try to refind the common ground that will bring them to unity in Christ. He was the victim of the worst sort of ecclesiastical politics at the hands of Cardinal Beaton – even John Knox saw the parallel with Caiphas suggesting that 'one man should die for the people'. Over the years, the Catholic authorities worked on the principle that making an example of one would deter the growth of Protestantism and until now that had worked. George Wishart was, however, different. His preaching was mostly a failure but his Christ-like kindness to plague victims in Dundee more than made up for the inability to popularise his mixture of Lutheran and Zwinglian thought. Roman Catholics could easily recognise in him the qualities normally associated with their canonised saints and martyrs. Suggestions that he was an 'English spy' have never been proved but in any case would not deflect from his essential witness of caring and fortitude. Protestants see him as one of the martyr saints who gave their lives in the footsteps of Christ Himself.

Two Protestant writers show the power of Wishart's witness. Knox contrasts Wishart's innocence with the scheming of Cardinal Beaton 'who was known to be proud' and Dunbar, archbishop of Glasgow 'who was known as a vainglorious fool'. He compares this to 'the accusation and death of Jesus Christ, when that Pilate and Herod, who before were enemies, were made friends, by consenting of them both to Christ's condemnation'. This he regards as remarkable because of the well-known incident when Cardinal Beaton and Archbishop Dunbar had their cross-bearers fight with one another to ensure their respective archbishops would enter Glasgow Cathedral first. Was it to be the archbishop of Glasgow in his own cathedral or the archbishop of St Andrews on the grounds that he was a cardinal and the Pope's legate? A good-going riot ensued, and Knox sees it as only being resolved when the archbishop of Glasgow 'sat next to the Cardinal, voted and subscribed first in the rank, and lay over the East blockhouse with the said Cardinal, till the Martyr of God was consumed by fire'. Knox goes on: 'After the death of this blessed martyr of God, began the people, in plain speaking, to damn and detest the cruelty that was used. Yea, men of great birth, estimation, and honour, at open tables avowed, that the blood of the said Master George should be revenged, or else they should cost life for life.'

Calderwood takes Knox's parallel with Christ's death a stage further:

[Two friars said] 'Mr George, pray to Our Ladie, that she may be mediatrix for you to her Sonne'; to whome he answered meekelie, 'Cease,tempt me not, my brethrein!' After this he was ledde to the fire with a rope about his necke, and a chaine of yron about his middle. When he came to the fire, he sat doun upon his knees, and rose again: and thrise he said these words 'O thou Saviour of the world, have mercy on me! Father of heaven, I commend my spirit into thy holie hands!' [He spoke to the people of the Word of God and suffering and declared] 'I know surelie, and my faith is suche, that my soule sall suppe with my Saviour, Jesus Christ, this night, ere it be six houres, for whom I suffer this.' [He forgave those who condemned him and] 'them that have forged anie lees upon me!' [and the executioner]. And, by and by, he was putt upon the gibbet, and hanged, and there burnt to powder.

Catholics have to ask – is this any different from their martyrs?

## 40   Cardinal David Beaton – monster or what?

One of the fascinations of history is to see how a popular 'identikit' picture of a character emerges which may be quite removed from the truth. One such is Cardinal David Beaton, who rose to have real influence under James V and in the succeeding regency to have real power once the pendulum had swung away from the English to the French connection. His long years in France as a diplomat were the key factor. He was responsible for the execution of the Protestant Reformer, George Wishart, before himself being murdered in revenge in his own room at St Andrews.

We begin with Sir David Lindsay's, *The Tragedy of the Cardinal*, in 1547.

> Off all Scotland I had the Governall's
> Bur my awyse, conductit was no thying:
> Abbot, Bysschope, Archbyschope, Cardinall,
> In to this Realme no hiear could I ryng.

George Buchanan's *History* in 1582 is the next stage:

> An arrogant priest and cruel tyrant who . . . destroys everyone who in the least offends him, however mean or wretched: who in Public promotes foreign and domestic hostilities, in private unblushingly unites meritricious loves in wedlock . . . at home revelling with prostitutes, and abroad rioting in innocent blood.

Principal William Robertson in his *History of Scotland* in 1759:

> By nature of an immoderate ambition: and insolence grew upon him from continued success . . . political motives alone determined him to support the one [Church of Rome] and oppose the other [Protestantism].

Robert Chambers in the *Biographical Dictionary of Eminent Scotsmen* in 1884:

A zealous churchman and the hired tool of France . . . who from his persecuting and selfish spirit was very generally detested.

David Hay Fleming in *The Reformation in Scotland* in 1910:

Desperate attempts have been made to whitewash this Ethiopian, to cover up the spots of the leopard: but all such attempts have proved, and must prove, futile. On 5 March, 1531, his son George and two daughters were legitimised . . . on 4 November, 1539 letters of legitimation were granted by James V to other three of the cardinal's brats.


In 1986, Dr Margaret Sanderson was quick to admit that he was vain and was driven by ambition to such an extent that he could resort to force when opposed, but she also showed that he was urbane, open-handed and charitable. Rather than pompous, he was in fact affable and effusive, winning people over by his charm. In terms of sexual morality, he didn't indulge in prostitutes and sexual licentiousness but instead had a stable relationship with Marion Ogilvie for twenty years, during which they looked after their children carefully and well. The expectation was that the church was on the point of recognising such relationships. His downfall was that he was a politician and disposing of George Wishart, who was an equally charismatic figure, seemed a necessary evil. Rather than his gloating about it, as Knox suggested, he was edgy and guilty: and at the end of the day it was English money that paid his assassins rather than popular support. A sad picture then, but a different one.

## 41 Catholic reform

Catholic reform is for many almost a contradiction in terms and yet the one thing that is abundantly clear is that almost everyone wished reform. The divide between Protestants and Catholics was largely about the speed of reform and whether it could be achieved within the existing structures or not. In the 1540s, Luther was dead and Protestantism was in retreat, with England the only really safe state. Calvin's work was still mostly in the future. Dr Michael Lynch of the University of Edinburgh describes it as an odd sort of vacuum; and into that vacuum on the Scottish scene there came from 1547 to 1559 a series of Provincial Councils aimed at reforming the church. The surprising thing about the statutes of these councils is that many of them would be almost indistinguishable from the reforming acts of the Protestant Reformation. Try these excerpts out for size: some are clearly Catholic; others would be shared concerns.

### Statutes of 1549

It is alleged that public scandals, both of greater and less enormity, are sometimes concealed and passed over by the deans and other visitors, for the reason that they do not blush to take bribes from concubine-keeping and adulterous persons, and so are made to defile themselves with such filthiness,this convention has enacted that the deans, before they hold office, shall promise upon oath faithfully to discharge its duties in every respect.

A cleric who does not wear the habit suitable to his order and standing renders himself unworthy of the honour due to that standing. [They are to renounce] dangling hair, full beards, and birettas laced with small cords after the fashion of the laity and secular persons: [in doing so] they create a public scandal in the church.

Rectors, vicars, curates and other priests are four times a year to cause to be publicly declared and denounced as excommunicate many of the lords temporal and othere secular persons and even churchmen too who infringe ecclesiastical jurisdiction and liberty.

Abuses are reported in which . . . the most sacred body of Christ our Saviour and the holy sacrament of the Eucharist is borne for the communion of the sick through streets and districts in an irreverent and secret fashion.

The concubines and wenches of ecclesiastics, and especially of priests who conceive by the same priests shall not be purified after childbirth unless by them sufficient caution be first produced that they will hereafter abstain from carnal connection and the suspicion of cohabitation.

In 1556, Cardinal Sermoneta reported back to Pope Paul IV the names of five bishops he felt were the most capable of effecting reforms: by the time of the Reformation, two of them were dead and another had fled to France. Whether they and others could have managed radical reforms to both the spiritual and financial structures of the church is a matter for conjecture, but they were certainly prepared to make these reforms.

## 42   Privy kirks – the quiet growth of Protestantism

The old myth that the majority of Scots were pushing stridently for the Protestant Reformation has given way to a clearer understanding of the idealism and quiet growth of enthusiastically convinced Protestants in Scotland in the 1550s. John Knox describes what we now know as privy kirks this way:

> Men began to exercise themselves in reading of the Scriptures secretly within their own houses: and variety of persons could not be kept in good obedience and honest fame, without Overseers, Elders and Deacons. And so began that small flock to put themselves in such order, as if Christ Jesus had plainly triumphed in the midst of them by the power of his Evangel. And they did elect some to occupy the supreme place of exhortation and reading, some to be elders and helpers unto them, for the oversight of the flock; and some to be Deacons for the collection of alms to be distributed to the poor of their own body. Of this small beginning is that Order, which now God of his great mercy has given unto us publicly within this Realm.

It's clear in privy kirks like this one in Edinburgh that was visited by John Knox in 1555 that Protestantism was spreading downwards from the nobles to the craftsmen and the apprentices. The numbers were small – small enough for them to meet in private houses – and persecution in the fifties was almost non-existent under Mary of Guise. Thus James Baron was an active Protestant who went to Geneva in 1557 and at the same time was Dean of Guild of Edinburgh Town Council and as such had the job of organising Catholic worship at St Giles. Calderwood's description of Edinburgh is even more specific:

> The professours of Edinburgh had their privat conventiouns this yeere, in the feilds in sommer, in housses in winter. William Harlaw and Johne Willocke were their teachers: sometimes Paul Methven and Johne Dowglas, alias Grant. They had their owne

elders and deacons . . . The small number increased daylie, until the time of publick reformatioun.

Dr Michael Lynch of the University of Edinburgh has identified some of those mentioned by Calderwood. George Small was an apprentice saddler; Michael Christison was a small merchant; Adam Craig was a journeyman in the goldsmith craft. There were nobles too, of course, but the place of the lower orders in the ranks of elders and deacons was never emulated in the years after the Reformation. When a list of 'the faithful brethren' of Edinburgh was drawn up in 1562, it took the form of a parade of the Edinburgh establishment with half of the top 100 taxpayers featuring on it, along with, of course, the Edinburgh lawyers, some thirty of them. There was no place, however, for the very ordinary working men who had figured so prominently in the privy kirks. The new kirk had taken on a new respectability which might be seen as some loss of earlier Reformation ideals.

Highly significant is the end of an appeal to the 'faithful brethren' of Edinburgh in 1562: middle class values seem already entrenched!

Heirfor we aboue chosin requiris euery broyer underwrittin in goddis name to subscryve at his name quhat he wil frelie contribut to the foresaid wark, nocht doubting but quha frelie and gladlie geive to this godlie wark god shall aboundantlie incresse his substance and blisse the samyn.

## 43   Burning of Walter Myln and the St Giles' Day riot

History is very often shaped by the fate of otherwise insignificant people. One such is Walter Myln, an obscure old schoolmaster, who was burned as a heretic at St Andrews on 28 April 1558. This was four days after the marriage of Mary, queen of Scots, and the dauphin of France. Knox accuses Mary's mother, Mary of Guise, of ordering the burning but this is highly unlikely both in view of Mary's preoccupation with the marriage and also because of her reliance at the time on a group of Protestant advisers. However, Archbishop Hamilton, as Knox also asserts, is much more likely to have been responsible since, although he was the author of a Catholic catechism, his cousin Châtelherault (Arran) was a Protestant whose son was languishing in a French jail for heresy. It may well have been his dreadful way of proving he was a good Catholic. On the other hand, a letter from Henry II of France to the Pope in 1559 suggests it may have been part of a move to introduce some sort of Inquisition to Scotland. However it came about, the reaction was accurately recorded by Knox.

> Which thing did so highly offend the hearts of all godly, that immediately after his death began a new fervency amongst the whole people: yea, even in the town of Saint Andrews began the people plainly to damn such unjust cruelty: and in testification that they would his death should abide in recent memory, there was cast together a great heap of stones in the place where he was burned.

More significantly, the Protestant lords and lairds determined that they had to act to safeguard Protestant preachers.

Later in the year, an event took place that Professor Ian Cowan of the University of Glasgow believes was because of a dispute between church and town council about the cost of a new statue of St Giles. This was to become, as Dr Michael

Lynch of the University of Edinburgh emphasises, a public proclamation by Edinburgh's hidden Protestants. The Catholic Bishop Lesley's account sees it as an occasion when 'al heretikes . . . suld recant in publik' but when instead 'sum heretikes steirit up sik a tumult schortlie' that they stole the statue of St Giles and 'brak the Image in peices'. Knox's account tells how the statue used in the procession had to be borrowed from the Grey Friars because the dispute about replacing the original statue had not been resolved and goes on:

> There assembled priests, friars, canons, and rotten Papists, with tabors and trumpets, banners and bagpipes. Then the idol was seized. There might have been seen so sudden a fray as seldom has been seen amongst that sort of men within this realm: for down goes the crosses, off goes the surplice, round caps corner with the crowns. The Grey Friars gaped, the Black Friars blew, the priests panted and fled: and happy was he that first got the house: for such a sudden fray came never amongst the generation of Antichrist within this realm before.

Yet another account comes from a pamphlet written in German but published in Geneva by the English Marian exile, John Bale. It was prompted by news which 'yesterday has been received by Mr Knox, a native Scotsman and famous evangelical Preacher' and in the tract further details emerged: not only was the statue of St Giles seized but also 'the ecclesiastical plate and religious banners, all resplendent and golden' were either snatched or smuggled away under the coats of 'the shameful papists and monks who fled through the narrow lanes'. Both the burning and the riot of 1558 became powerful symbols for the future.

## 44 Knox, the exile

In his *History of the Reformation of Religion within the realme of Scotland*, John Knox recounts the story of the siege of St Andrews after the murder of Cardinal Beaton in 1547 as if it were a dress rehearsal for the Reformation. Be that as it may, most of Knox's best-known written work emerged from his time in exile after the end of the siege. We have no real idea what the experience in the galleys did to his character but it must have been sheer horror. Many other questions are as yet unanswered. Why did he stay in the relative security of Edward VI's England at his ministry at Berwick when others like Spottiswoode returned to the challenge in Scotland in the fifties? At this stage of research we have no real answers. Puzzling too, or perhaps politic, is the fact that so many of his Berwick tracts were written for an English audience ('God was English' seems to come through!). Even his tract 'The First Blast of the Trumpet against the Monstrous Regiment of Women' was mainly directed south rather than having anything to do with Mary, queen of Scots, or her mother, Mary of Guise. When the Protestant Elizabeth came to the throne shortly afterwards he found it difficult to retract the 'law of God' and so Elizabeth always distrusted him.

After Mary Tudor came to the throne of England in 1553, Knox fled to the continent, though he returned to Berwick in 1555 to marry a Berwick girl and paid a short visit to Scotland where he was surprised and delighted by the progress of Protestantism in Edinburgh, Ayrshire and Angus. The whole period was clearly a time of deepening insights for Knox. Calvin's Geneva, Zwingli's Zürich and Basle all influenced a ministry for English exiles in Frankfurt-on-Main. However, a dispute about Edward VI's prayer book and kneeling at communion caused Knox to leave for a ministry in Geneva where he attached himself to Calvin, then at the height of his spiritual and political influence. Calvin joined Wishart as the twin inspiration of Knox's ministry, supplanting the influence of Zwingli which had shaped his ministry in Berwick-on-Tweed and his chaplaincy to Edward VI.

Another fascinating insight into Knox can come from the Berwick connection. His letters to his wife, mother-in-law and indeed to his 'dear sisters' in Edinburgh, whom he met in the privy kirk in 1555, all witness to his warm humanity and the fact that, despite the 'Monstrous Regiment of Women' tract, he liked women, was attracted to them and built warm relationships with them. It didn't affect 'business', however, for women in Knox's post-Reformation Scotland lost status rather than gained it. They were not even allowed to be godmothers at baptism and had no vote in kirk sessions. The 'trumpeter of God' (his description of himself) had another side to his character then and as a result, his letters to his mother-in-law provide some of the freshest and best accounts of the Reformation. Written after his visit to Scotland in 1555, they make it clear that following years of disillusion with Scotland he

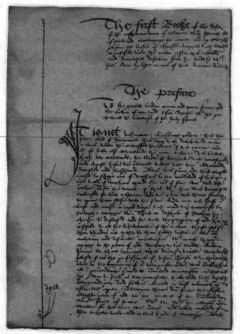

was now focusing his attention back on Scotland and in the process had been heartened by contacts with Scottish Protestant lords. These contacts would prove crucial in the future.

John Knox's "History of the Reformation of Religion within the realme of Scotland" *(from* Essays on the Scottish Reformation 1513-1625 *published by Burns).*

## 45 The revolt of the Congregation (1559-1560)

The Lords of the Congregation – as they're called – emerged as a loose coalition of lords and lairds on a broad anti-French platform. In late 1557 five of them issued a bond making their position clear after John Knox had reproached them for going back on their invitation to him to return. They 'undertook to renounce the congregation of Satan with all the superstitions, abominations and idolatry thereof' and 'to establish the most blessed work of God and His congregation'. The high-sounding rhetoric was balanced by practical political realism. Professor Gordon Donaldson has described it as 'the party of revolution' but it was arguably neither a party nor a revolution. It didn't even stay a Protestant movement as such for Catholic lords like the earl of Huntly joined it and kept his job for the crown. Lord Sempill was asked to join with the immediate acknowledgment 'peradventure you are not of our religion'. The Protestant earl of Morton, who had subscribed that first bond of 1557, laid low during the whole revolt.

The actual revolt got under way with Knox's help when the mob in Perth rioted after his sermon in St John's and looted the great Charterhouse and friaries. Jasper Ridley describes Knox for this reason as the only Reformer in the sixteenth century who was able, like Ché Guevara, to persuade the nobility to join the peasants in revolt. In fact the two movements were continuing in parallel not in tandem. The revolt of the Lords of the Congregation wasn't directly against Mary of Guise but against the advisers, the 'bloody wolves' of Knox's vivid phraseology. It began as a Protestant crusade but continued to become effective as a coalition of those who were worried by Mary of Guise's rule and the French connection, especially after the Protestant Elizabeth in England made the English connection more attractive. The Protestant earl of Argyll joined because he feared that Scotland would follow the way of Brittany and be annexed to France. The revolt became more conservative as its base broadened with Châtelherault (Mary's successor in the absence of an heir) and the Hamilton connection, with William Maitland of Lethington, the consummate diplomat, and with Lord James (Mary's half-brother), all joining later. The coalition enlisted the help of Elizabeth and so an English army and an English fleet laid siege to Leith. Mary of Guise died and France, torn by the gathering storm of religious civil war, was glad to agree to the Treaty of Edinburgh on 6 July 1560. Within weeks, the Lords of the Congregation had accepted the Confession of Faith as written by Knox alone, though they went on to reject a Book of Reformation and instructed a new drafting committee, made up of 'six Johns' – Protestant ministers of quite varying beliefs – to present a revised version to Parliament. This was what has come to be known as the *First Book of Discipline*. At the end of the day, as Professor Burleigh remarks in his history, the Reformers achieved only the legalising of their creed and the lords who helped them to achieve it were to make the road to the fulfilment of their ideals a long and difficult one.

Mary, queen of Scots, Fotheringay (from a painting by J. Duncan) (*by permission of the National Gallery of Scotland*)

## 46  Confession of Faith of 1560

When the Reformation Parliament of 1560 asked for a Confession of Faith, a remarkable document was produced in double-quick time, largely from the pen of John Knox himself. It was intended also as a proclamation of faith to be sent to other nations to let them know where Scotland stood. To this end, it paraphrased Matthew 24:14 at the very beginning: 'And these glad tidings of the Kingdom shall be preached through the whole world, for a Witness unto all Nations, and then shall the end come.' It is:

> the confession of faith professed and believed by the Protestants within the realm of Scotland, published by them in Parliament, and by the Estates thereof ratified and approved, as wholesome and sound doctrine, grounded upon the infallible truth of God's Word.

As such it's a relatively short document and it's far from being as rude about the Pope as the later Westminster Confession of Faith that is today the secondary standard of faith for the Church of Scotland. For that reason, it was seriously proposed by many at the 1986 and 1987 General Assemblies of the kirk that it should replace the Westminster Confession which is far more tightly and specifically composed in a rather narrow interpretation of John Calvin and as such has been the object of repeated conscience clauses for those who are asked on oath to subscribe to it.

The Confession asserts the authority of the 'Scriptures of God as sufficient to instruct and make the man of God perfect'. The notes of the true kirk are threefold: first, the true preaching of the Word of God; secondly, the right administration of the sacraments of Christ Jesus; lastly, ecclesiastical discipline, 'uprightly ministered, as God's word prescribes, whereby vice is repressed, and virtue nourished'. These are the notes of the true church as already defined in the Confession of the English congregation at Geneva. In general, the document isn't strikingly new or original but that is its strength. It expresses clearly and simply where Protestant faith was at this stage of development. Sacramental teaching is clear with infant baptism and the presence of Christ in communion but much is made of such points as the 'blind Papists . . . stealing from the people the one part of the sacrament to wit, the blessed cup'. Again, too, the context of the Reformation being pushed through by the Lords of the Congregation results in a strongly worded section:

> To Kings, Princes, Rulers and Magistrates, we affirm that chiefly and most principally the conservation (or Reformation) and purgation of the Religion appertains: so that not only they are appointed for civil policy but also for maintenance of the true Religion, and for suppressing of idolatry and superstition whatsoever.

Amid all the good things in the Confession, that section will hang like a shadow over relations between kirk and state for almost 400 years. Only in 1929 was it finally erased. One other contentious issue is the question of lawful ministry which it denies to be in the papistical kirk: 'We flee the society of the Papistical Kirk in participation of their sacraments, first because their ministers are no ministers of Christ Jesus: Yea they suffer women to baptise'! In place, ministers must be lawfully chosen by some kirk. Edward Irving perhaps sums up the Confession best when he called it 'the banner of the Church in all her wrestlings and conflicts'.

## 47 The *First Book of Discipline*: a social gospel

The Reformation Parliament of 1560 demanded from the 'six Johns' – of whom Knox was only one – a Book of Reformation. This in due course was entitled the *First Book of Discipline* and was remarkably impressive as an attempt to produce godliness – what today we would describe as an effective social gospel. It's true, however, that its first concern was discipline, for

> As that no commonwealth can flourish or long endure without good lawes and sharpe execution of the same, so neither can the Kirk of God be brought to purity neither yet be retained in the same without the order of Ecclesiastical Discipline, which stands in reproving and correcting of the faults, which the civil sword either doth neglect or not punish. Blasphemie, adulterie, murder, perjurie and other crimes capitall, worthy of death, ought not properly to fall under censure of the Kirk: because all such open transgressions of God's lawes ought to be taken away by the civil sword. But drunkenness, excess be it in apparel, or be it in eating and drinking, fornication, oppressing of the poore by exaction, deceiving of them in buying and selling by wrong, met and measure, wanton words and licentious living tending to slander, doe openly appertaine to the kirk of God to punish them as God commands.

This gave kirk sessions a wide remit with excommunication, sackcloth and ashes, and what have you.

Godliness also meant an educated people.

> Seeing that God hath determined that his church here in earth shall be taught not by angels but by men . . . of necessity it that your Honours be most careful for the virtuous education and godly upbringing of the youth of this Realm.

Thus provision was made to reinforce the system of grammar schools and 'colleges of the tongues': not surprisingly too, since two of the 'Johns' were from St Andrews, three universities were to be strengthened – St Andrews, Glasgow and Aberdeen – but St Andrews was to be 'first and principal'.

The Reformers didn't lose sight either of the dramatic 'Beggars' Summons', the eviction notices nailed to the friaries throughout Scotland, beginning with Perth (where there was local bad feeling). 'Let hym therefore that before he stollen, steill na mare: but rather lat him wyrk wyth his handes, that he may be helpefull to the pure.' Thus the *First Book of Discipline* enacted:

> Every several kirk must provide for the poor within the self . . . We are not patrons for stubborn and idle beggars who, running from place to place, make a craft of their begging, whom the Civil Magistrate ought to punish: but for the widow and fatherless, the aged, impotent or lamed, who neither can nor may travail for their sustentation, we say that God commandeth his people to be careful.

The ideal was established but down the centuries it was also one of the failures of the Reformation. Eight schemes were tried in Edinburgh alone during John Knox's time and all failed. Another problem was whether 'godliness' would ensure a good income, and as late as the nineteenth century Chalmers and Allison had still to argue that one out. We can see the seeds of that argument in the attitude to the beggars in the text above. Be that as it may, the only Poor Law provision in Scotland, from 1600 to the middle of the nineteenth century, was that based on an Act of Parliament of 1579 which sought to put into effect the principles of the *First Book of Discipline*.

## 48   Mary, queen of Scots: martyr or threat?

The story of Mary, queen of Scots, is a romantic and tragic one. As Dr Michael Lynch of the University of Edinburgh describes it, the popular version is a story of 'murder, sex and intrigue – with a touch of religiosity'. Did the coming of a Catholic queen to Scotland, a year after the country became officially Protestant by Act of Parliament in 1560 present a simple confrontation of the two religious approaches? It's been presented as such thanks to the oversimplification of Knox's *History*. However, the 400th anniversary of Mary's death instigated a whole range of research making the picture much more complex.

The first clue to the new picture is the fact that Mary was invited from being the newly widowed Catholic queen of France to be queen of Protestant Scotland by the very lords who had ensured that Scotland became Protestant. A bargain was struck so that she could retain her Catholic faith and have her Catholic chaplains at court but she in turn would have to respect the Protestant character of Scotland. This she resolved to do, as Professor Ian Cowan of the University of Glasgow observes, very much in the spirit of the Protestant King Henry IV of France who said that Paris was well worth even a Catholic mass. Were it not for the threat of becoming subject to France, the vast majority of her subjects would probably have welcomed a return to Catholicism. Politics, not religious conviction, were crucial; and Mary's treatment of the most powerful Catholic lord in the north, the earl of Huntly, and his death were either unfortunate byproducts of these politics (Lynch) or even, as Fr Allan White, OP, believes, a deliberate destruction perpetrated to convince the Protestant lords and Queen Elizabeth of England that she was sincere about a Protestant Scotland and sufficiently trustworthy to succeed to Protestant England.

Two other factors have to balance the political aspect. Dr

John Durkan of the University of Glasgow has shown from Mary's library that she was not only learned (as was likewise shown by Dr Marcus Merriman who researched her time in France) but also a convinced Catholic, a faith which she carried through the political intrigue of her time in England until she used it for her queenly role of playing the Catholic martyr with admirable courage and conviction. From 1565 onwards, and after her marriage to the Protestant Lord Darnley, the emphasis changed, however. There were popular pressures from the crowds who thronged to her masses rather than to Knox's services. After Darnley became a Catholic Mary tried to convert the other lords and not even the Protestant backlash following Rizzio's murder – or Darnley's – interrupted the process. At the end of the day, however, a mistaken marriage for political ends to Bothwell and the birth the previous year of Charles James, her son by Darnley, gave her enemies an alternative. In Loch Leven Castle she was forced to abdicate in favour of her son, now restyled King James VI. Exile in England followed, and her involvement in successive plots led to her execution by Elizabeth. She rose and fell because of politics: but her struggles with private religious convictions in that harsh world of politics are just as valid today in the world of Watergate and Irangate – and Britain.

## 49  Mary and John Knox

Knox's confrontation with Mary, queen of Scots, is one of the most dramatic personality clashes in the story of Scottish religion. It wasn't that Knox couldn't be close to women, because he was close to the 'dear sisters' of Edinburgh whom he met on his visit to the privy kirk of Edinburgh in 1555. Thus to Mrs Anna Locke: 'familiaritie once thoroughlie contracted was never yet brocken on my default'. In his dealings with Mary, however, there was a clash of two powerful personalities who were both claimants to ultimate power in Scotland. Mary was looked up to as a glittering queen, even by her Protestant subjects, and Knox was acutely aware of her attractiveness to so many. Thomas Randolph, the English Protestant ambassador, was clear about Knox: 'He ruleth the roost and of him all men stand in fear – would God ye knew how much!' He went on:

> Mr Knox . . . hath no hope [to use his own terms] that she will ever come to God or do good in the commonwealth: he is so full of mistrust in all her doings, words and sayings as though he were either of God's privy council, that knew how he had determined of her from the beginning, or that he knew the secrets of her heart.

In fact Knox preached against Mary on the first Sunday she was back in the country declaring that 'one mass is more dangerous than ten thousand armed enemies'. He was right: by 1567, 12,606 persons allegedly attended mass at Mary's chapel. Nevertheless his implacable hatred of her didn't go without criticism, even among the Protestant community. Thus Maitland of Lethington in the General Assembly of 1564:

> That is . . . wherein we find greatest fault. Your extremity against her Mass, in particular, passes measure. Ye call her a slave to Satan: ye affirm that God's vengeance hangs over the realm, by reason of her impiety: and what is this else but to raise up the hearts of the people against her Majesty.

It annoyed Knox that 'in presence of the Council she kept herself very grave [for she could play the hypocrite in full perfection]: but how soon that ever her French fillochs, fiddlers and others of that band got the house alone they might be seen skipping not very comely for honest women'. It gave him great satisfaction to reduce her to tears in their set-piece confrontations. Here's a snatch from one of them:

*Knox* Yea Madam, I offer myself further to prove that the Church of Rome is declined, and more than five hundred years hath declined, from the purity of that religion which the Apostles taught and planted.

*Mary* My conscience is not so.

*Knox* Conscience, Madam requires knowledge: and I fear that right knowledge ye have none.

*Mary* But I have both heard and read.

*Knox* So Madam, did the Jews that crucified Christ Jesus read both the Law and the Prophets, and heard the same the same interpreted after their manner. Have ye heard any teach but such as the Pope and his Cardinals have allowed? And ye may be assured that such will speak nothing to offend their own estate.

*Mary* Ye interpret the scripture in one manner, and they interpret in another. Whome shall I believe? And who shall be judge?

*Knox* Ye shall believe God that plainly speaketh in his word.

## 50   Ninian Winzet: Catholics find a voice

The story of Ninian Winzet is the story of a remarkable man who was a schoolmaster in Linlithgow from 1551 and who, when the Reformation came to Linlithgow in mid-April or mid-May 1559, proved himself to be one of the most courageous and capable defenders of the Catholic faith in the whole era. According to the Catholic historian, Bishop Lesley, he disputed with Knox about the Eucharist at the end of July 1559; with Patrick Cockburn about prayers for the dead; with Patrick Kinlochy, ex-canon of St Andrews and minister of Linlithgow, about the Eucharist and with Spottiswoode (superintendent of Lothian) in 1561. His *Four Scoir and Thre Questions* were the result of these disputations.

Thrown out of Linlithgow by the Lords of the Congregation, he turned up next at the court of Mary, queen of Scots, and travelled with her disputing verbally with John Robertson, another ex-priest, and George Buchanan the Protestant humanist, and in tracts with Knox and Edinburgh Town Council until his *Last Blast* was seized at the press of the printer John Scott in 1562 and Winzet had to flee Scotland. His later life sees him in Paris the following year and in England as confessor to Mary during her captivity at Sheffield (where he was suspected of being involved in the plotting and suffered a spell of imprisonment). He was in England briefly in September 1571, though his name was on the list of hunted priests, and then returned to Paris in 1572, finally ending his career with the Scots exiles in Ratisbon.

Fr Mark Dilworth describes him as the 'theologian of the lower clergy' and Dr Michael Lynch of the University of Edinburgh notes how he personalised the Reformation debate between Knox as the 'principal Patriark of the Calviniane Court' and himself, described in turn by Knox as 'Procutour for the Papists'. He challenged Knox directly to open debate:

Quhat auctoritie heifor haif ye for you to comptrol our souerane Lady and compel her Maiestie to reassure your privat opinioun of materis in religioun unknown to the haill Christiane Kirk afoir thir days?

Knox maintained a dignified silence: his status was enhanced by Winzet's attacks but in turn the 'coercioun' Winzet had to face and the seizure of his works showed that he too was feared and respected.

His first tract is a blistering attack on the old Catholic bishops and he told Mary that bad appointments had caused most of the trouble and yet, on the other hand, he clearly proves for Catholic readers that Knox is not a lawful minister for 'nane suld tak the honour of ministratioun of Godis Word and Sacramentis on him, except he be laichfullie callit thereto'. He defends the mass from charges of idolatry and shows that to deny Christ's presence is to brand accepted authorities such as St Augustine and St John Chrysostom as heretics. His argument is direct, learned and pithy – with all the characteristics of a good teacher – and he stands for admirers and critics alike as a shining example of learning and competence in the Scottish church, even at the lower levels of church life, in the years building up to the Scottish Reformation. His work covers the main areas of Catholic theology, comparing and contrasting the different approaches of Catholic and Protestant to good works, sacraments, ministry and reform: it's significant too that Winzet's tracts were written 'to achieve Reform'!

St Michael's Church, Linlithgow

## 51 Catholic resistance to conforming

The story of the Catholics after the Reformation is a story of the change from their constituting the majority of the population to becoming a tiny minority. Part of this change was voluntary, part was enforced: but where it was enforced, there was also resistance and, as with the Protestants before 1560, much of the resistance took place in little house churches. Naturally there was a good deal of ebb and flow about the situation. In the kirk's own analysis in the 1590s, one-third of the nobility had lapsed back into Catholicism. Even a stout Protestant like Lord Forbes of the north-east had two sons who became Capuchin friars. The sixth earl of Huntly agreed three times to return from papistry and on the second time the church threw a party in Aberdeen, with glasses being smashed in celebration of the return of the sinner. He then returned to Strathbogie and lapsed again, eventually dying peacefully as a Catholic in his own bed. The situation immediately after the Reformation had been described in a letter of the Jesuit, Fr Nicholas de Gouda, to the Jesuit General in 1562:

> Some of the nobles and men of means are Catholics. They hear mass occasionally, but secretly, in the privacy of their own houses . . . A large number of the ordinary common people indeed are still Catholics, but they are so oppressed by the tyranny of their opponents that they constantly sigh and groan, waiting for the deliverance of Israel.

As late as 26 July 1567, the Spanish ambassador in London is able to report that the communicants at Mary's private chapel in Holyrood had numbered 12,606 persons. Mary's confessor, Roche Marmerot, a Dominican friar, had them all registered. The kirk session was, however, a powerful instrument in wearing down opposition as it was local and was tightly disciplined. If someone was married in a Catholic ceremony, the children would be regarded as illegitimate. The records are full of characters who would be harassed in other ways. Fear of the plague in the sixties, and the constant worry about deepening poverty, made the loss of being able to pray for the dead a worry for many. In Elgin, a woman was accused of having prayed for the dead: she responded that she just 'had to pray for her faithful departed'. Another was indicted for 'praying on her child's grave'. The third time of being caught at mass could be punished by death but this rarely happened. John Carswell, superintendent in Argyll and author of a Gaelic version of the *Book of Common Order*, suggests that discipline and repression were only used 'against the stubborn'.

The records of the Aberdeen kirk session show the bishop's live-in wife Marjory Urquhart, getting into trouble:

> Mariore Urquhart being examinit befoir the sessioun of Aberdeen of hir religion, ansairit that schow wald nocht come to the communion, nor yitt to submit herself to the kyrk allegeand scho had sic ane pic on her conscience that schow culd nocht be fulle of this present religioune now in Scotland.

St Andrews kirk session in June 1561 had John Kipper arraigned 'for defending and mantenying of idolatrie, supersticioun, and Papistrie'. An interesting letter from Alexander Clerk, a Protestant town councillor in Edinburgh, speaks of a priest in 1565 'found guilty on his own confession', who had 'to stand at the market cross from 2 till 6 in the afternoon and then be sent back to prison. I am assured there was 10,000 eggs spent upon him: and at his down taking . . . 300 or 400 men with batons would have killed him had he not been taken away back to prison'.

## 52   The new worship: communion and the word

It's always been an attractive oversimplification to say that the Reformation of 1560 in Scotland changed Scottish worship from being centred on superstitious ritual to being centred on the sermon and the Word of God. The focus certainly changed dramatically but many things continued as before. The sermon dominated every service whether it was baptism or communion, though, with the stress on graduate ministers, people in the early days sometimes had to wait two or three weeks before a minister was able to preach at their service.

Right from the first Confession of Faith, stress was laid on communion in the form of wine as well as bread, not just for the celebrating minister (as was always the case) but for all the congregation as well. Not having this was interpreted as deliberately denying the laity their proper place. The unleavened bread was dropped in favour of a more realistic meal, tables were brought into the pewless kirks and the bills for wine escalated dramatically (extant accounts record six and a half gallons for one kirk). The service often started at four in the morning (for the servants) and continued until noon. Its shape was much as today. Knox insisted that the minister should sit at the same level as the congregation and should share the elements, as in a meal. Clearly communion became less frequent but the practice of Easter communion remained. Thus in Monifieth at Easter, ten times the normal congregation turned up (600-700) and people were admitted to communion if they were able to give evidence that they knew the Lord's Prayer, the Ten Commandments and the Apostles' Creed.

Most churches were purged of statues and ornaments though ways were found to circumvent this suppression. St Ninians in Aberdeen had a lot of Catholic ornaments in 1574 'just to keep out the draughts'. None the less, a great number of wall paintings and carvings, for example in Guthrie Collegiate Church, survive to this day for it was only in the seventeenth century that Presbyterians began to lay down that walls should be bare and whitewashed. The first churches after the Reformation clearly showed the liturgical centre to be the pulpit rather than the communion table – Greyfriars (1620) and the Tron (1647), both in Edinburgh, are good examples .

Baptisms also took place in the churches, normally in a simple ceremony after the sermon. There were godparents and they and the father had to recite the Apostles' Creed. Despite the opposition of the Reformers, the burials of lairds continued to take place in the churchyard. And since the ordinary people retained a deep fear of death, aggravated by the prevalence of plague which was very much seen to be a sign of God's anger, funeral services full of concepts of the judgment of God were prestigious events in the community.

In general then, it can be said that the Sunday service was seen not so much for worship as such but rather as an occasion for teaching and learning. This was extended by the afternoon series for children where Calvin's Catechism was taught section by section. Scots began to learn their faith with a vengeance!

## 53 The new worship: marriage, saints, music and the Sabbath

In the early days of the Scottish Reformation, matters were far from being as dour as they were to become later. The emphasis on listening to the Word of God and on the minister's expounding that Word of God took away the colour of ritual. The general character of the Sunday was not yet the Scottish 'Sabbath' of later centuries but Sunday markets were stopped and ale-houses were shut at the time of services. In Dundee children were not allowed to play in the kirkyard during services – that would presume, however, that they were allowed to do it the rest of the day! Mungo Craig in Glasgow and James Roy in Elgin were both condemned by the kirk session for playing the bagpipes on a Sunday.

Marriage by habit and repute was still legal in Scotland, therefore it was more often the rich who were married in the kirk. Banns were called and it was encouraged for the marriage to take place on a Sunday with preaching accompanying it. As time went on, however, those who were austere began to feel uneasy about the festivities attached to weddings.

Festivities of the saints didn't die out all at once despite the Reformers' strictures. In spite of its claim to be producing the 'most perfect reformed church', the Geneva Prayer Book of 1562 still had a calendar of moveable feasts of saints – and of the many feasts which remained in the *Book of Common Order* were those of the Purification, Annunciation and Conception of Mary, and saints' 'fairs' everywhere you go! Ian Paisley or Jack Glass would find it difficult to believe! The lack of biblical names, except in ministers' children, is striking and shows a continuing place for saints in aiding people's way of thinking. Andrew Melville, a generation later, still believed in angels.

The Psalms, however, were to be sung unaccompanied. In 1564, the Psalter was published with the financial backing of an Edinburgh merchant who was a client of the earl of Moray and was based on the French Huguenot version rather than on Knox's. While this was the staple aid to public worship, it was balanced by a studied encouragement of private devotion with the prayers and instructions for examining children 'before they be admitted to the supper of the Lord', which were added to Calvin's Catechism, published in the same year. Prayers were 'to be used in private houses everie morning and evening'. Some organs were removed but some instrumental music was retained. The *First Book of Discipline* laid down the general rule: 'In some churcheis the Psalmes may be conveniently sung: In utheris, perchance, they may not.' The commissioner of Nithsdale had occasion to complain that in Dumfries, seeing neither he nor the reader 'would read nor use doctrine upon these dayyes, brought a reader of their own with tabron and whistle, and caused him to read the prayers'. Aberdeen conceded, but only in 1574, that 'the organs, with all expeditioun, be removit out of the kirk'.

The Scottish Reformed tradition then was in compilation right up to the 1630s when confirmation was found of the hatred of set prayers (they were seen as Catholic or Anglican); the imposition of extempore sermons as opposed to the written; the growth of conventicles; and the reabolition of saints' days, for example by the Glasgow Assembly of 1638. At this point only can one say that there is a mature Reformed tradition.

## 54 The first General Assemblies of the kirk (1560s-1590s)

There had been national church councils before the Reformation but at the heart of the kirk today is the General Assembly of the Church of Scotland, not only the highest court of the church but also the great debating stage for affairs of church and state in Scotland. In 1560, it didn't just take a new approach but it witnessed, at least hesitantly, to the great theological ideal of equality by baptism in the decision-making of the church. With Queen Mary in France, the Assembly was at first freed from worrying about the relationship with the crown and so it grasped the opportunity to make itself a parliament relating to the church with all the important elements of the three estates represented. The Lords Spiritual – the bishops – were there, on and off, until 1690, but balancing them and ultimately taking over from them were the representatives of the parishes, ministers and elders alike. The Lords Temporal were there, right down to the local lairds and up to the Privy Council. There were still shire and burgh representatives but they tended to represent rather narrowly their own constituency interests. The shire representatives were gradually seen to be superfluous but the burgh representatives lasted until 1929 when there evolved the present arrangement of ministers, elders and a Lord High Commissioner to represent symbolically, but rather powerlessly, the interests of the crown.

They were stirring and heady days: political power struggles and religious idealism all mixed up in a cauldron of confused ideas. The lines of the Treaty of Edinburgh were clear: proscribing the Pope's authority, abolishing the mass and adopting a Protestant Confession of Faith that owed more to Luther and Zwingli than to Calvin. One hundred lairds and nobles were at the Reformation parliament which met in August 1560. We know that the Catholic bishops were outflanked and that the assembly debated for twenty-six full days with very little legislation at the end of it all and without any minutes having been taken. The parliament of 1584 would meet for only four days and produce thirty pages of legislation. It was a revolution that changed in the making. The first Moderator was probably a Zwinglian, John Willock of Glasgow, so having an ordinary minister in the chair was the first success. Much about the first assembly is shrouded in mystery but we know that it met somewhere in Edinburgh on 20 December 1560 and that forty-two ministers and lay commissioners attended 'to consult these things which are to send forward God's glorie and the weill of his Kirk in this Realme'. The early concerns were practical: the appointing and overseeing of ministers, finance (how to make do with only about one-tenth of the old church revenues) and discipline in such matters as divorce. The early Assemblies took place twice a year (often deliberately sitting on Christmas Day), and this mainly in Edinburgh, though they did move around a bit. A good idea, since at that time the Protestant bishop of Shetland had to go to Lerwick, then Hamburg and eventually to Leith. The commissioners often complain today, but their journey then was really something to complain about!

## 55   The ministers of the kirk

One of the justifiable attacks of the Scottish Reformers concerned the poor quality of the parish priests in Scotland and one of their great successes was the quality of the ministers who succeeded them. Of the six Johns who wrote the *First Book of Discipline*, John Knox had a quite outstanding mixture of experiences both in Geneva and with French Calvinism; John Willock, recognised as 'Primat of thair religioun in this Realme', had experience in Edward VI's England and in Denmark; John Erskine of Dun, provost of Montrose, who set it all off by writing to Mary of Guise, was purely Scottish but highly effective: two Johns were from the leading Catholic Reformers of the fifties and the sixth, John Row, was an expert canon lawyer who had just come from Rome. In 1560, Scotland had 1,000 parishes but with the Reformers' insistence on quality, there were only about 250 with ministers by the end of the sixties with readers helping out in the others. At the centre were an élite of fifty who knew one another well and shaped the future together. The leading ministers were well paid, from £200 to £300 in 1560 and £1,400 Scots in the 1640s. 'They lived like lairds' and were able to lend money to the nobility: John Knox was able to make a loan to his father-in-law, Lord Ochiltree. On the other hand, however, they were expected to work hard for their money. A typical rural parish was 750 strong but Knox in Edinburgh had to cover 12,000 with one other minister and a reader. Communion started at four in the morning with the servants and continued in successive waves until noon, and then the children were taught in the afternoon. In Perth, there was one minister for 6,000 and when another was appointed in 1585, the kirk session noted that they would expect a weekly household visit! In Monifieth, kirk records show that the minister had to spend much of his time working at the sermon and visiting the sick. In the south-west, the memory still remains of Samuel Rutherford who in the 1630s worked so closely with his congregation that he transformed their education in the faith as well as ushering in what could only be described as a quiet social revolution.

Some of the lesser known characters are worth a mention. Mr William Gray in Angus excommunicated the local laird, Lennox of Shandford, for living in sin with a girl. The laird responded by marching up the aisle with drawn sword and had to be restrained from killing him. The records of the Privy Council show another minister who was attacked while riding to church. Again, too, they show Mr Andrew Milne of Fetteress having to enlist the Privy Council against the harassment of the Roman Catholic heir of William Douglas of Glenbervie. Yet another was John Durie, an ex-Benedictine, who was banished in 1582 for criticising Esmé Stuart, the Duke of Lennox, for his friendship with French courtiers and for visits to the red-light district of the Cowgate in Edinburgh. He came back to Leith when the heat died down and then entered via the West Port, deliberately re-enacting the entry of Mary, queen of Scots. He had gathered 400 supporters by the time he reached the Netherbow, then 700 and finally he rounded off with 2,000 fanatical supporters singing Psalm 124. The watching duke of Lennox 'reave his beard for anger: he was more affrayed of this sight than anie thing that ever he had seene before in Scotland'. Such was the power of the new ministers of the kirk: quite a contrast from their place in society today!

## 56 The kirk session

The kirk session is, with the Reformed ministers, the great achievement of the Scottish Reformation. It's almost unique in Europe as a link between the minister and congregation and between churches. It emerged as a real agency for social change, drew Scotland together and revolutionised society. In saying all that, however, it had a Janus face. The first face looked to the care of the poor and the sick, while the second face looked out at the sins of society, expecially the sexual variety. In the records of kirk sessions, it is easy to lose count of the cases of fornication and adultery that brought miscreants to the stool of repentance with the sackcloth and public acknowledgment of sin which that involved. It has to be said that it was mostly women who were forced to appear and that members of the establishment were often reconciled in private but the practice certainly did something for discipline in society. We would now see it as wrong and as opening the door to oppression and abuse but the religious intensity that gave birth to it was indeed reminiscent of the early centuries of the church. That particular form of primitive repentance ritual and welcome back to the church has gone, but the kirk today has to ask what has been put in its place.

One of the disappointments of the kirk session was that, unlike the privy kirks of the 1550s, the apprentices didn't get the chance to become elders. In the towns, the burgh establishment (usually rich merchants and lawyers) made up the elders with lesser characters as deacons. In rural areas, the well-heeled farmers tended to dominate rather than the cottars. Again, too, the *First Book of Discipline* laid down yearly elections but in most cases the elders carried on in office. One exception was in Edinburgh where genuine annual elections carried on in the seventies, even if lawyers topped the polls and the office of deacon was distinctly less sought after. In some ways then it was an adjunct to the establishment but it also

proved to be the breeding-ground for radicalism, especially
among the craftsmen who were to become in the eighties the
Melvillian politicians who built the kirk's Presbyterian future
against the odds. Being an elder was both good and bad for
business. It meant closing up on Sunday, but it also meant
social and therefore commercial prestige.

Stories abound in the records of kirk sessions. Most offences
are to do with family life and forcing Catholics to toe the line.
We find a woman reproached in Elgin because 'she just had to
go to pray for friends departed', another because 'she had to
pray on her child's grave'. William Anis in the Canongate
couldn't come to communion 'because his heart geared to the
mass'. The third time of being caught at mass could mean death
but it happened to few. As John Carswell of Argyll put it,
discipline was kept for the 'stubborn'. And there were amusing
stories. William Williamson, a baker in Perth, was had up for
baking great breads at Yule (Christmas) and thus encouraging
superstition; likewise a schoolmaster in Haddington for
baptising a cat according to the Reformed tradition; and also a
crowd for saying a service over a minister's horse when he rode
into Paisley and it dropped dead. The whole of life is in those
records: the good, the bad and the ugly!

Ordination of elders, 1891 (from a painting by J.H. Lorimer) (*by permission of
the National Gallery of Scotland*)

## 57 The Jesuit mission: persecution reversed

On the continent, the Jesuits were seen as the storm-troopers of what was called the Counter-Reformation, the renewal of the Roman Catholic church from within which had the added purpose of making it more attractive in order to persuade Protestants to return to the church of the Pope and bishops. Scotland never 'suffered from' or 'benefited from' such a confrontation as other places for even those who joined the Society of Jesus from Scotland were very often assigned to work in Austria, Poland, France or even Italy: these countries were much higher up the scale of priorities than Scotland. All priests were forbidden to say mass but many of the old ones were pensioned off to live out the rest of their lives in peace. Successive Acts of Parliament acted against 'Jesuits and seminary priests'; the new priests trained abroad and returned in the 1580s to work in secret.

The first Jesuits who came to Scotland had only been passing through in the 1540s on their way to Ireland to combat the problem presented by Henry VIII's imposition of a Protestant bishop of Armagh. They wished to replace him by a Scot, Robert Wauchope of Niddrie Marischal near Edinburgh, who was, quite remarkably, a blind bishop. After the Reformation, one of the main Jesuit groups to be active was associated with Robert Crichton, bishop of Dunkeld, who remained a clandestine Catholic and escaped detection for most of the time, except for one occasion when he was put on trial for offering mass. His encouragement meant that a whole group volunteered from his area for the Jesuit mission. Edmund Hay of Meigle went from St Salvator's in St Andrews to Louvain, and continued his friendship with Andrew Melville, the great Reformer, whom he met in Paris; he did likewise with Thomas Smeton, a Jesuit who defected to Protestantism and became Melville's successor as principal of the University of Glasgow. Things are never as black and white as they seem. James Tyrie of Drumkirk, James Gordon (son of the earl of Huntly) and James Gordon of Lismore were among the many who lasted only a short time before being caught and banished. William Murdoch of Drumkilbo in Perthshire distinguished himself by masquerading for almost twenty years as a schoolmaster and a physician. He led, of course, a hunted life, except for spells with the earl of Huntly when he openly debated with the local minister. John Ogilvie has in recent years been declared a saint for his death as a martyr after being caught, but most priests were just banished. They lived a stimulating life on the run and brought books with them to strengthen Catholics in their faith: the library of Robert Abercrombie has given a vivid insight into these imports. The story of a Glasgow burgess, Andrew Hathaway, and his wife, Jane Pollock, illustrates that lay Catholics also faced banishment for helping priests. When Fr George Mortimer, after an exciting time of comings and goings one step ahead of the law, was finally caught hiding in the slates of their house, they were banished and travelled to Strabane in Derry by what must have been a favourite escape route for the laity, because the Protestant archbishop of Glasgow tried several times to persuade the Irish to put a stop to Catholics hiding there.

The Jesuit mission of the 1580s then was a tremendous encouragement to those who had been hanging on to their faith in the Catholic version of the pre-Reformation privy kirks which so sustained the tiny minority of Protestants in the 1550s. Too little and too late would be the version of hindsight but the Pope had other priorities in the divided Europe of the day – and Scotland was too small and too far away to get top priority.

## 58   Andrew Melville

Andrew Melville has very often been accused of returning to his native Scotland and disturbing what had been established at the Reformation of 1560. In fact he was invited back in 1574, as one of the most distinguished scholars in the sixteenth century, by the Protestant bishop of Glasgow to revive the moribund university. The son of a minor laird, Melville attended the University of St Andrews and graduated in 1564. He studied in various universities abroad and, like Knox, drew most inspiration from Protestantism in France and Geneva. Theodore Beza, who succeeded Calvin in Geneva, was a particularly formative influence. As principal of the University of Glasgow, Melville transformed it into a place respected throughout Europe for its theology and arts. In the same position in St Andrews in 1580, he made St Mary's College a centre of excellence. More importantly, he tried to revise the teaching methods so that each student did not just have a regent supervising all the studies but was taught instead by specialists in each field: Hebrew, geography, history and mathematics, as well as theology.

Coming from Beza's Geneva, however, he brought ideas of what we now know as Presbyterian government of the church, ideas which were to lay the foundations of a 150-year struggle between church and state. Both in intellectual input and in personality, Andrew Melville was to be the epicentre of that struggle during the reign of James VI of Scotland and I of England. Great men are rarely easy to live with and Dr John Durkan of the University of Glasgow points out that personality clashes didn't make Melville's task any easier. The first dispute was with Regent Morton, who scoffed at his 'overseas dreams', but then Morton as a Douglas had a vested interest in the power of the crown, especially as one of his kinsmen was archbishop of St Andrews (1572). Thomas Wilson was a student of Melville for five years but married into the family of one of Melville's enemies, Archbishop Adamson: his assessment was that Melville was 'better at ruling schools than ruling kirks and commonwealths'. Again, too, Melville provoked bitter opposition at the University of St Andrews and there was a confrontation with the archbishop which came to a head in 1583: but power struggles in universities are rarely amicable even today!

When James VI came into power he began a lifetime of conflict with Melville. In 1584 Melville had fled into exile in England for twenty months to avoid being imprisoned in Blackness Castle for seditious preaching. Later, at Falkland Palace, Melville plucked the king's sleeve, reminding him that there are 'twa kings and twa kingdoms in Scotland' and in one of these kingdoms, he was just 'God's sillie vassal'. A sermon at St Andrews was reported to the king in which Melville had to hammer home the point that the king couldn't try him before a presbytery court had the opportunity to do so. James was furious at this appeal to what he saw as a new-fangled type of church organisation. That organisation, however, was dear to Melville's heart and to achieve it he had demanded quite remarkable hard work and application from the committee with whom he worked for two years to produce the *Second Book of Discipline,* which laid out the principles of Presbyterian rule. After James took over in England, Melville lambasted the Anglican Archbishop Bancroft in open debate before James, again defending the same principles. He ended his days in exile but he left behind a legacy of Melvillian ministers, a radical party who ensured the ultimate triumph of the Presbyterianism that is Scotland's pride today.

## 59   The clash of crown and kirk (1584)

The Scottish Reformation of 1560 left unanswered a great
many questions. The role of the Lords of the Congregation in
pushing matters along blurred the lines between the role of the
lay state and the organisation of the church. The power that
brought the Reformation into being wished to shape its future.
In the Reformers' plan, Scotland was divided into ten districts
which would have ten superintendents. The *First Book of
Discipline* spoke of the superintendents as 'a thing most
expedient for the time', which Dr Michael Lynch of the
University of Edinburgh describes as one of the most
contentious statements in Scottish church history. 'Expedient'
could be thought of as meaning 'necessary'. These
superintendents had the role of ruling and admitting to the
ministry, though that must be balanced by the fact that they
were not seen to have a sacramental role and also by the fact that
men like Erskine of Dun and John Winram spoke of themselves
and other ministers as bishops. The superintendents were
given then a limited but defined role.

In the whole of his rule during the minority of James VI,
Regent Morton worked at the principle of ensuring that the
crown had the right to appoint these superintendents. Andrew
Melville provided the intellectual strength for the kirk's
instinctive struggle against that right. His committee, which
included such characters as the lawyer Clement Little (who left
his books to help establish the University of Edinburgh),
worked for two years producing the *Second Book of Discipline*
in 1578. It clearly distinguishes civil government from church
government, the latter deriving from God in Christ. Regent
Morton refused to accept it. Harking back to the Reformation,
the *Second Book of Discipline* accepts that the magistrate or
godly prince may purge the kirk but maintains that when the
kirk is properly established, it should be content to strengthen
its four offices: (1) pastor, minister or bishop; (2) doctor or

teacher; (3) presbyter or elder; (4) deacon. All have to function within their particular flock by whom they are elected.

The sensational coup known as the 'Ruthven raid', when a group of Protestant nobles seized the young James VI in 1582 and had their actions endorsed by the General Assembly as an 'act of reformation', left an indelible impression on the mind of the young king. He escaped a year later and a royalist backlash went into full swing. Control of the newly established University of Edinburgh (made possible first of all by the bequest of the Catholic Bishop Reid of Orkney before the Reformation) was snatched back from the radical Presbyterian ministers and their supporters just a week before it was due to open in October 1583. A parliament which met in Edinburgh in May 1584 amidst strict security – with radical Presbyterians temporarily forced out of town – restored the authority of the crown and took away the authority of the thirteen newly established presbyteries, which were cast in the role of a 'fifth column' endangering the safety of the nation. These were the 'Black Acts' of 1584 and this was the beginning of a long struggle which continued even after Presbyterianism was re-established by the 'Golden Act' of 1592. By cleverly arranging times and places of the meetings of the Assemblies (allowing people like 'the drunken Orkney ass' to dominate), James restored his right to appoint bishops and when he went to England even ensured that they would have Anglican reordination. He seemed to have won until he went too far with the Five Articles of Perth in 1618 when he sowed the seeds that in Charles's reign would ensure the conflagration of opposition to bishops that would assure Scotland's Presbyterian future.

## 60 'The godly prince' – James VI

The idea of the 'godly prince' developed among the Reformers of the sixteenth century as they wrestled with the corruption of the church as they saw it: the barriers to reform represented by the Pope and the 'princes' of the church; and their moral reservations about any sort of revolution against God's established authorities. It derives too from the medieval idea of the 'divine right' of kings and indeed the Old Testament concept of the prophets that God uses even pagan rulers like Cyrus to achieve his divine purpose. Each sect saw the 'godly prince' in different ways but all saw the Reformation as a Reformation from above with the king becoming Protestant and imposing his faith from above.

Scotland of course had no 'godly prince' in 1560 and none during the sixties when Mary, queen of Scots, was in charge of Scotland. The birth of Charles James, the future James VI, in 1566, with Mary being deposed in his favour in 1567 gave the Protestant nobles their chance and they followed it through resolutely. The name Charles with its Catholic associations was dropped. James was taken charge of so that he could be trained in his role as 'godly prince'. The leading humanist and teacher of the sixteenth century, George Buchanan, who had left his mark as teacher of the earl of Moray thirty years before, was appointed to be James's tutor and ruthlessly instilled in James the combination of Plato's idea of the philosopher prince with the Protestant idea of the 'godly prince'. James took this seriously and debated whether he should exercise his role within the Episcopal or Presbyterian tradition. He grew up to be perhaps the most literate Scottish king, or British one for that matter, of all time. He wrote many books, both spiritual and secular and, despite accusations of having flirted with the Catholic faith, remained a staunch and convinced Protestant. At a time when Protestantism was in retreat on the continent – and godly princes were in short supply – he was hailed as the great hope for Europe.

By the end of his rule, however, many weren't so sure. George Buchanan was to the left of the Scottish Protestant church but lost influence by the viciousness of his attacks on the reputation of James's mother, Mary. James hadn't seen her since he was one year old and indeed feared she might interfere with his rule – but she was still his mother! He didn't take kindly either to the Ruthven raiders kidnapping him and trying to get him to ensure the kirk was ruled by presbytery and Assembly. Andrew Melville in debates at Falkland and later in London, annoyed him intensely by his lack of due deference either to his learning or to his role as 'godly prince'. Basically, however, James's vanity and his own view of the role of 'godly prince' made somewhat hollow his proclamation of the kirk in 1590 as 'the sincerest kirk in the world' and the English church as having 'an evil said mass in English, wanting nothing but the liftings'. When he took over as James I of England, the 'godly prince' exiled Melville and not only undermined the power of the General Assembly of the kirk (which he'd already largely done) but reintroduced real power to the continuing episcopacy and ensured that they were legitimised by the Anglican English bishops. The nauseating flattery of the English clergy could be said to have turned the 'godly prince' into a true 'Head of the church'. The Five Articles of Perth – with kneeling for the sacrament of communion – were for many the ultimate betrayal.

## 61 Early seventeenth-century worship

It's often been said that, in addition to the ideal that faith should lead to and shape the way people pray, the manner in which people pray shapes what people believe. Early seventeenth-century worship was reaffirming the values held in common in both Episcopal and Presbyterian strands in the post-Reformation established kirk. A fascinating insight into how far it had moved from Catholic days is presented in a 'Seven Dayes Conference betweene a Catholic Christian and a Catholic Romane' about 1620, which is printed in Cowper's *Works*.

*Prot.*   Good morrow sir, are you ready to go?

*R.C.*   When you please.

*Prot.*   What church will you goe to, or whom of the Preachers desire you to heare?

*R.C.*   Make you the choyce. I will accompany you . . . what is this the people are going to doe?

*Prot.*   They bow themselves before the Lord, to make a humble confession of their sinnes and supplications for mercy: which you will have openly read out by the publike Reader. Now when it is done, what thinks you of the Prayer?

*R.C.*   Truly I think there is nothing in it but whereunto every good Christian should say, Amen: and it hath done me much good to see the people with humble reverence, sighing and groaning, accompany the Prayer up to God. But what go they now to do?

*Prot.*   Everyone is now preparing (as you see) their Psalmbook, that all of them, with one heart and mouth, may sing unto the Lord.

*R.C.*   . . . What does the Reader now, is he making another prayer?

*Prot.*   No, yonder booke, which he now opens, is the Bible: you will heare him read some portion of holie Scripture . . . Those are the three exercises which are used in all our Congregations every Sabbath, one houre before the Preacher come in: first prayer, then Psalmes, then reading of the holy Scripture. And by these, the hearts of the people are prepared the more reverently to hear the Worde and you see that all is done with great quietness, devotion and reverence.

R.C.  I see that indeed . . . But what are they doing now?

Prot  You heare the third Bell ringing . . . at the end of the Bell ringing, the Preacher will come.

All in all, the services had a recognised stereotype which could be developed either in what we know as the direction of rigid Presbyterian worship or Episcopal ritual. Gilbert Burnet, later in the century, gave a fine description of the central quality of the Presbyterian ministers:

They used to visit their parishes much, and were so full of the Scriptures, and so ready at extempore prayer, that from that they grew to practise extempore sermons: for the custom in Scotland was after dinner or supper to read a chapter in the Scriptures: and where they happened to come, if it was acceptable, they of the sudden expounded the chapter. They had brought the people to such a degree of knowledge that cottagers and servants could have prayed extempore. I have often overheard them at it . . . I was astonished to see how copious and ready they were in it. By these means they had a comprehension of matters of religion, greater than I have seen among people of that sort anywhere.

## 62 Witchcraft

The heyday of witches or rather the persecution of people thought to be witches, comes after the Reformation. The first Act against witchcraft was passed by the Scottish Parliament in 1563 and the man probably behind it was the Protestant and highly educated noble, the earl of Moray, the half-brother of Mary, queen of Scots. The first witch burned was at St Andrews where, chained to a pillar, she had to listen to a sermon by John Knox in the process. There's been a great deal of speculation as to why witches should have become the scapegoats of the uncertain and the unexplained in life and the suggestion has been made that it resulted from the Calvinist concentration on the inner wickedness of man which wasn't taken away but only covered over by the merits of Christ. Be that as it may – and more research will have to be done on the subject – the kirk session certainly was usually the first court the witches came to before being passed on to a higher secular court. It was normally at the in-between stage that we find evidence of torture (the terrible boots that crushed the legs and so on; and even in some cases the torture of husband and children in front of the witch) and sleep deprivation (resulting in the devil and Mary hallucinations which are recorded) and witch-pricking (by frauds who made a good living out of the supposed identification of witches by sticking pins into their bodies at parts where there was or wasn't sensation). The normal method of execution was strangulation followed by burning.

The witch hunts came in waves throughout the most Protestant areas of Scotland – the Lowlands, the East Coast, Fife and Lothian in particular – and the worst of these were in the 1590s, towards the end of the 1620s and between 1649 and 1662. The last execution was at Dornoch in 1727 but though the Act of 1563 was repealed in 1736 witch belief lingered on for at least a half century more. As Burns makes clear in 'Tam o'

Shanter', the Scottish witch didn't always follow the English pattern of the old crone on the outskirts of the village but could be a winsome wench – though more normally a widow of about middle age, probably ill tempered, and with a sharp tongue and living on her own smallholding. Sometimes the only suspicion of her arose from the practice of primitive medicine or a spot of midwifery which went wrong but at other times it was a matter of finding a scapegoat. Extravagant estimates of how many were burned range from 3,400 to 30,000 but 1,000 is now the more sober, though still frightening, estimate. In the 1650s, no mature woman living in Fife or East Lothian could have felt safe from being accused. Examples abound. Apart from the North Berwick witches (who frightened James VI by causing a storm at sea when he sailed to Denmark to marry Anne and who revealed to him what he had been saying to his new bride on their wedding night), witches didn't normally have covens but were individuals who, as in Tranent in 1659, were caught in cycles of accusation and counter-accusation. Accusations of eating babies and so on were rare. The most common charge was that of having sex with the devil in the house or in the field. Reading accounts like those of Agnes Pogavie at Liberton or Marioun Grant at Aberdeen leaves one with the impression of simple, imaginative women caught in a mixture of fear, religious practices concerning Mary and the saints and nightmares about the devil. Ninety per cent were women but Major Weir of Edinburgh is a well-documented exception. His black staff and cloak, and his 'heavenly gesture . . . more angell than man' led at first to crowds praying at his house but subsequently to his indictment and death. It was dangerous to be different in times of fear and suspicion.

## 63   The Five Articles of Perth: James VI goes too far!

James VI had taken over as James I of England in 1603 and so
by the time he paid his first visit back to Scotland in 1617, he'd
had many years of flattery from the Anglican clergy to reinforce
his view that Scottish worship should be brightened up by
being brought more in line with English worship. His attack
was two-pronged and it's hard to know which infuriated people
more. He restored his chapel at Holyrood, to make it more
suitable for Anglican worship, with what were seen as 'papish
decorations'. Then, since he had failed to have the Assemblies
of the kirk abolished, he had pushed through at a General
Assembly at Perth what are now known as the Five Articles of
Perth. Eighty-six persons voted for obedience to the king's
wishes with forty-nine against: among the latter were most of
the ministers. The clergy of Edinburgh, however, sided with
the establishment to win the day but in doing so set up the
conflict that was to lead to riots twenty years later. The radical
ministers of the south-west were infuriated and they were to
find allies from the social revolution now affecting Edinburgh
itself with the doubling of its population. Meantime the five
articles became law though the bishops were to find major
problems in imposing them. They ordained the celebration
with appropriate scripture readings of Christmas, Good
Friday, Easter Sunday, Ascension Day and Whitsunday (all
feasts that are now commonplace in the kirk); baptism in
private houses when necessary and 'Holie Communion in
private houses to sicke and infirme persons'; the 'catechizing of
young children of eight yeers of age, and presenting them to the
bishop to lay hands upon them, and blesse them'; and, most
controversially of all, that communion 'be celebrate to the
people humblie and reverentlie kneeling upon their knees'.
Despite the way the articles have been caricatured, three of
them were reviving the normal pattern of church life in the early

years of the Reformation; the feasts were debatable and the kneeling certainly seemed to many to imply papist belief.

The reaction of Edinburgh's kirk session encapsulated existing tensions and pointed the way to future conflict. There was a furious debate with John Meine, a simple deacon, on one side, and Alexander Clerk, bailie, ex-provost and royalist on the other, giving a foretaste of the Covenanting struggles. They began by tossing obscure Scripture phrases at one another. 'Have ye read the Sixt of the Acts? Ye sould serve at the tables. Ye think your selfs verie wise. Wold to God we had als meikle wisdome amongst us all foure as everie one of yow thinks ye have.' Then things deteriorated. Alexander Clerk said, 'Hold your tounge. I command yow silence.' John Meine replied, 'Ye may not lawfullie command me silence in this place. Ye are but a sessioner heir, Sir. Ye may not raigne over us.' And the rejoinder: 'Ye are bot a verie false knave. Ye are but a gouke, Sir, I sall fasten your feete, Sir.' John Meine answered, 'I can beare all that, Sir, and all that you can doe to me, and more too, Sir. Bot I will not hold my toung so long as they speake to me.'

It's worth noting that the lowly deacon appeals now to what will be the new alliance between the Presbyterians of the lower classes and the ministers. That is the alliance which produced the Covenanters.

## 64 Jenny Geddes or somebody?

One of the most carefully nurtured myths in Scottish church history is the story of Jenny Geddes spontaneously lifting her hassock and throwing it at the minister when he used Laud's Prayer Book for the first time on 23 July 1637. She got the credit for the very real riot that started that morning in an account written twenty years afterwards; but no trace of her can be authenticated. To make matters worse, it has now become clear that the riot in St Giles when Charles I tried to impose Laud's (English) Prayer Book on Scotland was carefully planned and in fact similar disorders also took place in the other city kirks. In Greyfriars, the minister had to stop preaching because of the tumult and the unedifying spectacle is recounted of his being chased through the streets by a crowd of cursing women and his cursing back just as strongly! In St Giles, the dean retired up the steeple for safety but the bishop was foolish enough to venture out and was roughed up by the mob. He returned in the evening with an armed guard!

The planning of the events took place at a meeting in Edinburgh attended by a number of ministers along with parishioners of more humble state and some women. The women were chosen to lead the riot on the basis that it would then appear more spontaneous. We don't know if the nobility were present at the meeting but we do know that many of them would be known to be supportive of the plan to resist the king's rather autocratic introduction of something as central to worship as the Prayer Book. The resistance wasn't planned as a result of studying the book but rather because it was English and 'smacked of Popery'. This last charge was ignited by the constant stories spread in Scotland about Catholic guile and atrocities in the Thirty Years' War, then raging on the continent.

Dr Walter Makey, former Edinburgh City Archivist, observes that the most significant aspect of the riots is that even though the royal Privy Council and the magistrates of Edinburgh were present at the service in St Giles, none of them attempted to quell the uproar. The king was then being resisted at the highest level. A token gesture was made of holding some of the rioters for a week but there was no inquisition as to who was behind it, and they were quietly set free. Dr Stevenson of the University of Aberdeen sees the planning as going a stage further. The movement snowballed on a national level in a carefully organised way. The first stage was riots; then a wave of petitions from many parts of Scotland, ranging in a broad arc from Ayrshire to Fife, especially from the ministers; lastly, another wave of petitions from the lairds and nobles. In a matter of weeks the king had lost control.

Who then did the planning? The credit seems more and more to be given to Alexander Henderson, a Melvillian minister born in Fife of a tenant farmer who bought his own farm. He was a superb public speaker and preacher and skilfully used the political situation to weld together an alliance of ministers and feudal aristocrats to resist Charles's attempts to 'anglicise' the Scottish kirk. He lived on the fringe of trouble right into the difficult years of the English civil war and Scottish involvement in it. He, rather than Jenny Geddes, was perhaps the real hero!

## 65 The diarist of the revolution: Archibald Johnston of Wariston

Lawyers have played a prominent part in the story of the kirk from the earliest days of the Reformation. No less than thirty of the 160 'faithful brethren of Edinburgh' who made up a subscription list in 1562 were lawyers and a lawyer topped the poll in the first surviving record of an Edinburgh kirk session election (1574). They came to prominence along with the lairds, the merchants and the ministers but outstripped them all. In 1565, they had as much wealth as all the craftsmen of Edinburgh put together and by the 1690s they had more than the combined wealth of all the city's craftsmen and merchants. Despite this wealth, they managed to be exempt from paying taxes, along with the poor and the ministers, and yet some of them still remained poor.

Archibald Johnston of Wariston was one such impoverished lawyer. Born the son of a merchant whose wife was the daughter of the most famous feudal lawyer, Sir Thomas Craig of Riccarton, he married the daughter of another famous lawyer, Sir Lewis Stewart, although she was only fourteen (he was twenty-one) and her face 'al spoiled by the poks'. In their short marriage of nine months, he promised 'never to glaume nor glucke on hir befor folks' with her 'vowing never to disobey [him] in any compagnie'. Like her, he took life and religion very seriously. In bed on the Sunday after their wedding in St Giles, he examined her on her knowledge of God and was 'ravisched with her ansuears and blessed god for hir'. After she died, he began his diary in which he tells how he 'roared', 'youled pitifully', and 'skirled' in his devotional torments. The diary could easily have been dismissed as the record of a religious fanatic who verged on complete madness but, instead, it unfolds as a running commentary on the combination of religious idealism and practical legal strategy which made the revolution of 1638 effective against all the odds. His prayer life

130

was intense, his coping with the death in 1638 of the son of his second marriage was saintly, and the partnership with his competent wife at his farm in Wariston – though turbulent – was a fine example of true Christian partners struggling with their difficulties and their faults (he had a terrible temper and recalls how he had to go back to a poor man to make his apologies). From the imposition of the Prayer Book in 1637 ('that black doolful Sunday') he worked long and hard for the Presbyterian cause: he was the principal author of the National Covenant (Wed. 28 Feb.: 'that glorious marriage day of the Kingdom with God') and was driven on by his vision of a perpetual contract between the people of Scotland and 'Scotland's God'. His production of the old records of the General Assemblies turned the whole mood of the Glasgow Assembly of 1638 to its condemnation of episcopacy. Made Lord Wariston by Charles I in 1641 and then Lord Advocate by the Covenanters in 1646, he later established a working relationship with Cromwell's administration of Scotland, despite his reservations about Cromwell's tolerance. With the Restoration, he fled abroad but was arrested in Rouen in 1663 and, although obviously broken in mind and body, was hanged on 22 July.

His piteous cries were a tragic echo of what his vision of God's people and God's Scotland were to mean for the dwindling band of Covenanters in the years of persecution and yet an enduring challenge to all who take seriously, both in law and implementation, the relationship between church and state in Scotland – or any other country.

## 66  The Covenanters at war (1639-1650)

After Charles I's crude attempt to impose Laud's Prayer Book,
the campaign was built up ruthlessly both against the 'Popish
tendencies' and against the Protestant bishops who were seen as
agents of the king. The National Covenant was written by
Alexander Henderson, an Edinburgh minister, and Archibald
Johnston of Wariston, and was signed first at Greyfriars Kirk in
Edinburgh on 28 February 1638. The Covenanters then
proceeded to a General Assembly in Glasgow which was packed
with their followers: there hadn't been an Assembly since 1618
and James VI had filled the previous ones with his supporters.
Bishops were banned, popish practices were eliminated,
Presbyterianism proper was re-established but the king's role
was still acknowledged. None the less, Charles decided that this
was rebellion. He prepared to invade and the Covenanters
raised the first of their amazingly successful armies. Their
success depended partly on being underestimated but mainly
because their religious zeal was infectious, and they combined
this with practical measures. They brought the hardened,
professional Scottish mercenaries back from the continent and
gave them alternate ranks with the landowners, who rather
amateurishly used to dominate Scottish armies. Their first
expedition in 1639 forced Charles to agree to a parliament to
ratify the actions of the Glasgow Assembly and their successful
revolution perhaps marks the first time in Scottish history that
ministers achieved real power (though Dr Stevenson of the
University of Aberdeen believes that they were losing power by
1640/1641). In 1640, the Covenanters invaded England and
freed Charles to call the fateful 'Long Parliament'. When civil
war finally broke out, the Scots responded to Parliament's
appeal for help of November 1642 in return for the acceptance
of Alexander Henderson's newly drafted Solemn League and
Covenant, a religious bond which would have made England
Presbyterian too. On this basis, the Scots played a key role in

the parliamentary victory of Marston Moor in 1644. The execution of Charles I in 1649 shocked them and so we find the Covenanters at a later stage doing deals with Charles II which were to provoke Cromwell's invasion and their first defeats.

Two characters dominate and illustrate the period. One was the commander-in-chief of the Covenanters, Sir Alexander Leslie, a good organiser but not a great general, who was kept in the post for far too long. As earl of Leven, he came to believe that God was so much with him that he could go on to rule Scotland, England, France and Rome. At the battle of Marston Moor, he fled for miles thinking the battle was lost only to discover eventually that the reverse was true. One of the chaplains saved his blushes: 'God had decided He himself would be the general.' He typified Covenanting attitudes when things went wrong: 'What was God playing at . . . why were they being defeated by God's enemies?' His response was that they must become more and more godly. The other character was James Graham, earl of Montrose, who began as a Covenanter but, either because he felt they were going too far or because ambition took him in a new direction, subsequently led six successful campaigns against the ruling Covenanting group. He was eventually executed as 'the cause of their misfortunes' when he failed to rally support for Charles II. He may well have deserved his unfortunate end but many others in this period were ruthlessly persecuted by the Covenanters in power – a situation that was just as sadly to be reversed in years to come.

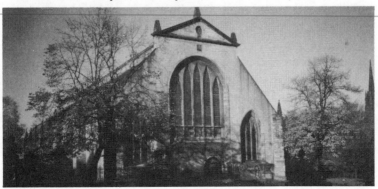

Greyfriars Kirk, Edinburgh

## 67 The Westminster Confession (1644)

The Westminster Confession of Faith represents at one and the same time the high point of the power of the Covenanters from Scotland over events in England and also the irony of an English Confession of Faith becoming – as it is – the standard of faith secondary only to the Bible in the kirk to this day. Each minister still has to swear to uphold the substance of the faith, though a conscience clause is now respected as to certain aspects of it. It emerged from the conjunction of the Scots' wish to impose Presbyterianism on England and purge all remaining 'Popish elements' and the English Parliament's attempt during the Civil War to reform the doctrine, worship and government of the Church of England. To this end, the English Parliament nominated a parliamentary advisory commission of 121 ministers and thirty laymen from all strands of opinion except the Anglican (who remained loyal to the king). After its first meeting on 1 July 1643, the Church of Scotland responded to an invitation to send representatives: thus men like Alexander Henderson, Robert Baillie, Samuel Rutherford and George Gillespie had an important influence on the documents, even though they feared the Independents and Baptists of Cromwell's army just as much as the Anglicans.

The document is more Calvinist than Calvin himself. Its language is more extreme against the Pope than the Scots Confession of Faith it replaced. Part of that would be due to the Melvillian ministers from Scotland but the English influence – as Dr Duncan Shaw, the former Moderator, has researched – had its origins in Holland among the followers of Bullinger and Zwingli. It essentially perverts Zwingli's thinking when it states the doctrine of 'double predestination'. This takes to its logical conclusion the idea that we totally depend on God to be saved: God therefore was seen to predestine some to heaven and some to hell. God, however, as Dr Shaw remarks, is outside of logic. Then again, the Westminster Confession is very legalistic in that rather than the group covenant of the early Reformers (between God and his people) it stresses the individual contract between God and man. This poses real difficulties in trying to assess the influence of the Confession. Did it result in Scottish religion in the following centuries neglecting the social dimension of religion – and its responsibilities – in favour of individual piety? It is arguable and the argument is worth assessing as a background to some of the church debates of today.

The final irony of the Westminster Confession is that, though drafted in England and accepted in Scotland, it was never implemented in England for by the time it was completed, Cromwell and the English Parliament had no need of assistance from the Scots against the king. As to the Scottish Covenanters, their finest hour had gone.

## 68   The kirk divided: Resolutioners and Protesters (1650s)

The tragedy of the Covenanters was that they were so imbued with the idea that God was on their side that when things went wrong, they divided one against the other and destroyed themselves. In practical terms, they had overstretched their resources by fighting a war on three fronts: in England for the Parliamentarians; within Scotland against Montrose; and in Ireland against the Roman Catholic rebels. Some concluded that they had been unrealistic and so when Charles I seemed to promise them all they wanted in church affairs, and it became clear that the Parliamentarians would not, the aristocrats persuaded the Scots to enter into what was called 'The Engagement', only to be roundly defeated by Cromwell at Preston. Recriminations followed with the ministers declaring that the army had failed because it needed to be purged of all elements that were not godly. The nearest thing to theocracy emerged. When Charles II came to Scotland and pledged himself to the Covenant, the army was made up of Protesters alone: all royalists and aristocrats were excluded. The Resolutioners who 'resolved' to draw together all elements had been set aside. The Protesters were in the minority but had their strength in the south-west of Scotland. Thanks to the Act of Classes, the earl of Argyll and the Protesters had made sure that their army was totally 'pure' and this made their numbers relatively small when faced by Cromwell's invading forces. It was an amazing act of faith but it led to disaster at Dunbar on 3 September 1650. The extremists were discredited, but a dwindling minority carried on the struggle from the south-west and slipped past Cromwell to final ignominy at Worcester on 3 September 1651. This was Cromwell's 'crowning mercy' and General Monck proceeded to subdue Scotland.

Cromwell's commonwealth was built on toleration for everyone except Catholics and those in favour of prelacy. In

Scotland, the majority, the Resolutioners, were mostly glad to compromise with his rule but the Protesters were irreconcilable, both with Cromwell for his toleration of sectarians and Baptists and with the Resolutioners. The English rule of the fifties saw the kirk weakened by the constant wrangles of the two factions and at times even two Assemblies until the latter were forbidden to meet again after 1653. Even ministers of the broad vision of Samuel Rutherford were trapped in the diminishing and ever more rigid 'sectarian church of the godly'. The 1650s then brought out of the tensions of the Covenanting ideals the seeds of separate Scottish Protestant churches in the future. Their faith lives on as a challenge to a less religious society and to every argument about the relationship of 'Church and Nation'. Many still believe that this was the golden age of Christian faith in Scotland.

## 69  'Sectaries and Baptists' (1650s)

Cromwell's ideal was to unite the people of Scotland and England in one commonwealth and one government, with Scotland enjoying free trade and having thirty representatives in a British parliament. It didn't come to much in political terms but his toleration of smaller Protestant sects split the kirk of the time on the lines of its own factions and introduced various other groups from England which were regarded as sects. The squabbling of the kirk's ministers allowed him to shut down the one separate national institution which might have resisted his great ideal – the Assembly of the kirk. Dr Walter Makey, former Edinburgh City Archivist, likens Scotland at the time to Russia from the 1920s until the 1980s. There was a weariness which bred disinterest: people were fairly happy with the secure rule of Cromwell and left the ministers to their arguments. He feels Cromwell himself didn't really worry what sort of church Scotland had as long as it wasn't opposed to him, but others, he says, would disagree and would point to the fact that churches as well as other buildings were used as barracks and even stables as evidence of Cromwell's contempt for the kirk. What is certain is that he was determined to end the church's role as a symbol of Scottish politics: some in Scotland were glad of that but the Covenanters bitterly resented it.

Among the 'sects' that came to Scotland with Cromwell's army were Baptists, Quakers (stressing the practicalities of this life) and millenarians like the Fifth Monarchy Men (who expected an imminent second coming of Christ). Scotland had its own variations: one landowner on Deeside was reputed to have tried to walk on the waters of the river. Then again, there were the Independents whom Cromwell favoured. Because many admired Cromwell's Puritan godliness, groups of Independents established themselves: one such group was in Aberdeen where the university principal and several ministers joined. Cromwell didn't like the Baptists but there were a good number in his army and Leith Baptists can look back to this time for their origins. Quakers, too, were officially disapproved of, but not actually suppressed. Dr Stevenson of the University of Aberdeen has traced a fairly strong presence in Aberdeen. Dr Walter Makey traces back the beginnings of the Congregational Church to the theological background of the Puritan revolution in England. The congregation was stressed as 'a collection of like minds getting together' and as such the congregation might well find being in 'the established church' a major inhibiting factor. Here, too, the conventicle – that was to be so important for the Covenanters in their time of persecution – was provided with a theological rationale.

Each group arising from this period has enriched the history of the Christian church in Scotland in their own way down through the centuries. Each deserves that we assess and learn from their insights. This short book cannot do them justice.

## 70 Freemasonry in the seventeenth century

Until recently, Freemasonry was thought to have originated in England in the eighteenth century. In fact there were many lodges in seventeenth-century Scotland and it seems to have emerged in Scotland about 1600 in the groups of stone-masons who were left outside society after the Reformation destroyed the monasteries that were their base. Craft guilds had come late to Scotland so they had a lot of vitality left in them at the time of the Reformation: their spiritual ideals and rituals led straight into those of Freemasonry. William Shaw, the 'King's Master of Works' to James VI, drafted the organisation and injected Renaissance wisdom into the medieval thought patterns. Dr Stevenson of the University of Aberdeen, whose research is central to the new understanding of Freemasonry, admits himself totally puzzled as to why it was not suppressed. William Shaw was even a Catholic. The ritual, the secrecy and the giving of moral guidance all seem naturals for kirk condemnation. One minister's ordination in 1650 was questioned on this basis but he was accepted for the integrity of his 'mason's word'. One of the most bewildering groups was in Aberdeen late in the century for it was both Quaker (by definition opposed to all ritual, even the sacraments) and Freemason, and yet tolerated in both Presbyterian and Episcopal Scotland! By the 1640s, there is evidence of courtiers in Edinburgh beginning to join: quite a contrast from the original stone-masons, though it should be added that one legacy of its origins in Scotland is the fact that there are still more working-class masons in Scotland than elsewhere. By 1700, representatives of all classes – nobles, ministers, craftsmen – were found in the still small-scale but significant lodges. By the end of the seventeenth century, Scottish Freemasonry had spread to England, then to Europe and around the world: Robert Burns, George Washington and Mozart were all masons. In the 1730s, the papacy outlawed continental atheistic Freemasonry as a secret society working to destroy belief in God. Perhaps that condemnation was the reason why Protestant churches took until the 1980s to start making negative pronouncements.

The original appeal of Freemasonry has still to be clearly established: Dr Stevenson's work continues. Was ritual attractive to church people newly deprived of ritual in their church services? We don't know. What we do know is the more social side of its attraction. It gave continued identity to displaced stone-masons in the sixteenth century and by the late seventeenth century was attractive to the new phenomenon of the coffee house which was the catalyst for all kinds of social groups. Another factor may well have been the search across the whole of Europe about 1600 for secret societies in order to find an agency that would somehow bring unity to the apparently hopelessly divided Christian world. The defence today of Freemasons – that their morality doesn't interfere with Christian morality and their ideas of God have no specific religious content that would contradict any individual religion – may well have been used in the past to keep them free from the oversight of the kirk session: or it may have been the secrecy in an age when there were no 'investigative journalists'!

## 71   Bishops restored: Sharp, Burnet and Leighton

It's difficult to imagine Protestant bishops in Scotland today and easy to forget that they existed in one way or another from 1560 right up to 1638 when the Covenanting General Assembly abolished them and substituted full Presbyterian government. The ban on bishops lasted through Cromwell's military rule of Scotland even though the General Assembly was proscribed for most of the period. The year 1660 brought Charles II to an ecstatic welcome in London and waiting for him was James Sharp, minister of Crail, who had been sent by Robert Douglas and a group of ministers from the less extreme Resolutioner party of the original Covenanters. His job was to keep an eye on the situation and try to safeguard the interests of the Church of Scotland: he was fairly optimistic because one of Charles's closest advisers was Lauderdale, a deeply committed Presbyterian. He had immediately to report that the Solemn League and Covenant which would have made England Presbyterian was dead: bishops were in the ascendant with royalty restored. Scotland, they felt, would be different. There were expressions of joy and gratitude in Edinburgh by most but the Protesters, however, drew up a 'supplication to the king', and this was immediately identified as a threat. Their leader, James Guthrie of Stirling, was left to languish in prison. The Estates were summoned for 1 January 1661, and lasted until July. By then the marquis of Argyll, James Guthrie and Johnston of Wariston were doomed: and only his previous death saved Samuel Rutherford from the same fate. Despite broadly-based objections in Synod, Charles proceeded to impose bishops on Scotland.

Three of these bishops present us with a series of enigmas. They were Sharp himself, who returned from his English mission as archbishop of St Andrews to be immediately accused of having sold out his commission to do his best for the Presbyterian kirk. Professor Cowan of the University of

Glasgow believes that – despite his bad reputation – he was a mild man who was only dragged slowly and reluctantly into the persecution of Covenanters. In fact, his initial tolerance allowed the movement to grow in the east. In the end, however, his contempt for the extremism of the Protesters led to his murder on Magus Muir. In Glasgow, Burnet came in a little later but was so extreme in persecuting Covenanters and introducing Anglican-style worship that he had at one stage to be removed from Glasgow, only to return to power with Lauderdale at a still later stage. The greatest puzzle of all is Robert Leighton. He is revered by many Presbyterians and Episcopalians to this day. His library, still housed at Dunblane, is a huge and astonishing collection of the most gifted intellect of the age. He was a reluctant bishop who, at first, would only accept Dunblane because it was poorly endowed and unimportant, but later took Glasgow. He offered his resignation as soon as persecution started but then returned and took his part. He designed and worked for 'a scheme of Accommodation' to bring the opposite sides together and sent his curates (labelled 'apes') out to persuade and discuss. He eventually resigned to end his days in quiet piety in England. Despite appearances, Professor Cowan believes he was a 'trimmer', bending his sail to the prevailing wind. He could, however, have been a saint, but the surrounding violence seems to have sadly tarnished his halo.

Dunblane cathedral

## 72   The Calvinist landlord: Clerk of Penicuik

Sometimes history becomes focused on a single person whose life seems to highlight the issues. One such in the seventeenth century was John Clerk of Penicuik. He had an impressive colliery at Loanhead, built from the money his father had made in the Paris Art Market in the 1640s selling Catholic baroque art. The mine brought him in more than £400,000 Scots a year: an almost incredible fortune. Part of the profits he used as an 'improving landlord' in the pattern that was to become commonplace a century later; for intellectual ideals, large sums of money were invested at a great loss in 'land improvement'. John Clerk's story, however, is important for quite different reasons. In some ways, he is the perfect example of the Protestant work ethic (work is good and if persevered in brings God's blessing) as it develops into the combination of neo-Calvinism and capitalism that was later to mark Victorian Scotland.

Between 1692 and 1720, John Clerk made 109 personal covenants with God: the National Library of Scotland still has this account of them entitled 'Register of all my personal covenants with God in Christ through the Holy Spirit'. He carefully devised for his miners a minimum of twelve hours' production a day (which of course meant many more hours' work). It seems by our standards inhuman and un-Christian but in fact was a 'caring Christian crusade' within his lights. Right from the *First Book of Discipline* of the Reformed kirk, a distinction was made between the 'deserving poor', such as widows and the lame, to whom poor relief was given, and the 'undeserving poor', the vagrants whom the barony courts, presided over by the local laird, would force to work. A flood of such beggars resulted in the century after 1625. In the 1640s the cause was not so much failed harvests but plague for in 1645 alone, 20 per cent of the population of Edinburgh and 20 per cent of the population in a six-mile radius died as a result; for many dependants only forced labour or vagrancy remained.

Colliers, fishermen and salters – as in an Act of Parliament in 1679 – were regarded as beneath the possibility of Christian outreach. Coal owners were allowed to force vagrants to sign up to work for them for life and John Clerk did this for all his workers in a personal bond to him and to the Lord. John Kirkwood for example had to declare:

> I bond and obey me then to study Christianity more, to learn the catechism, to be more frequent at prayer, to be at my work daily by four, to obey John Clerk and to go to bed by eight at the latest.

John Clerk then saw himself as driving out immorality and building godliness. Cost and profit didn't come into the equation. It took the twentieth century to see clearly that such godliness was un-Christian – and no union would in any case have stood for it!

## 73 Conventicles and Covenanters: brother against brother

Perhaps the saddest tragedy of post-Reformation Scotland is that the worst persecution came not from the Catholic-Protestant divide but from Protestant against Protestant on both sides of the divide concerning the Covenant in the 1670s and 1680s. The duke of Lauderdale ruthlessly turned on his former colleagues, exploited their divisions with 'Indulgences' and pursued into their conventicles (the hillside gatherings for worship) those who maintained the extreme Covenanting position that England as well as Scotland should become Presbyterian with the church severing all connection with the state. The Protestant Bishops Leighton and Sharp got caught in the persecution mania and Burnet also took it up enthusiastically. The Pentland rising of 1667 consisted mainly of humble people and badly armed peasants and this was to be the pattern. After the crushing defeat at Bothwell Brig, many were detained in Greyfriars churchyard in Edinburgh. Most were released but 200 were deported to the West Indies and perished when their transport ship was wrecked in the Orkney Islands. Lauderdale gave way to James, duke of York, the heir presumptive – a Catholic but determined at this stage on toleration. Peace settled in the country but not in the south-west. Richard Cameron rode into Sanquhar in Dumfriesshire on 22 June 1680, renouncing Charles Stuart and denouncing 'the duke of York, that Papist'. Cameron was slain in 1680, Donald Cargill was executed in 1681 and James Renwick in 1688. Led at first by the old soldier Tam Dalyell of the Binns, the 'Killing Time' went on from 1680 to 1688. About a hundred were executed and many more were transported.

The cemeteries of the south-west have vivid inscriptions to those such as James Harkness 'who endured twenty-eight years persecution by tyranny, did him pursue with echo and cry, through many a lonesome place': and to women, as in Wigtown with a 'virgin martyre here murthered for owning Christ Supreme, Head of the Church and no more crime but not abjuring Presbytery and her not owning Prelacy'. Characters abound. The Reverend James Fraser writes movingly of his three imprisonments on the Bass Rock, Blackness and Newgate before returning to Culross as minister. John Nisbet in Harthill, who was executed on 4 December 1685, testifies to his faith but also to his belief that 'Scotland's covenanted God will cut off the name of the Stuarts' and that all the armed rebellions were godly and the compromises offered immoral. Other accounts such as that of Alexander Reid of Broxburn were simple human testimonies, but he too sees the downfall of James VII as the 'hand of God'. As for Tam Dalyell of the Binns, 'he lived so and died so strangely, it was commonly believed he was in covenant with the devil'. On the other side of the argument, the Lord Advocate, Sir George Mackenzie – known as 'Bluidy Mackenzie' – was a highly educated man with reasoned arguments for all that was done to suppress the Covenanters whom he sees as 'the madcap zealots of this bigot age'. 'My heart bleeds,' he says, 'when I consider how scaffolds were dyed with christian blood and the fields covered with the carcasses of murthered christians and it's probable there were more damned by unprepared deaths in the fields than were saved by peepy sermons in incendiary churches.' He felt that they had brought the tragedy upon themselves. History is still divided on that judgment but the courage of the martyrs is a challenge both to those who agree with their views and those who do not.

## 74 Presbyterianism established

The alliance of Charles II and the earl of Lauderdale looked as if it had ensured Scotland would have bishops rather than presbyteries as the organising unit. Then came James VII of Scotland and II of England. He was Roman Catholic but affairs were so much in turmoil after the Covenanting wars – and there were so few Roman Catholics around – that the fact that James gave Roman Catholics positions of power didn't cause too much upheaval. In 1687, however, he allowed Catholics freedom to worship and extended it to Presbyterians. This in fact undid the work done since 1660 as Presbyterians poured out of the established church and set up opposition. The ground was prepared then for the forced abdication of James by events in England.

This came about because of mounting alarm, probably unfounded, that James was intending to restore Catholicism. The heirs to the throne were William and Mary of Orange, then champions of Protestantism on the continent. The appeal went out to William 'to do something about that old uncle of yours, your father-in-law'. Since James was an old man and in poor health, many felt that there was little point in an upheaval. All that changed, however, when James acquired a young wife, Mary of Modena, who then promptly gave birth to a son who would be heir in William's place. The Catholic threat became suddenly real: William of Orange landed in England and James lost his nerve and went to pieces.

The news of William's landing made the unchurched Presbyterians in the west and south-west decide on revenge. Rabbles commenced in November aimed at ejecting the Episcopal clergy and at Christmas organised bands of men and women succeeded in forcing out upwards of 200 clergy with threats and violence. Claverhouse raised a rebellion for James but was defeated and killed by the Cameronian regiments at the battle of Killiekrankie. As the legend significantly put it, he 'was killed by a silver bullet, because only a silver bullet could kill the agent of the devil'. Covenanters didn't forgive traitors from their ranks very easily. William would paradoxically have preferred an episcopal system in Scotland, if only for the sake of unity throughout his kingdom, but Claverhouse and the Jacobite landed gentry made the triumph of Presbyterianism inevitable. The Revolution church settlement of 1690 confirmed the Westminster Confession of Faith and the government of the church by kirk sessions, presbyteries, provincial synods and general assemblies. A commission was set up to 'try and purge out all insufficient, negligent, scandalous and erroneous ministers'. Even patronage was abolished, except for town councils. To all intents and purposes, the Covenanters gained all their aims but the Cameronians refused to accept the settlement because the state imposed it: and the Episcopalians were driven out of the established church to begin the Episcopal church as we know it now. There was still a divide about the line of the Tay within Scotland. The north was Episcopalian and it took the 1715 and the 1745 rebellions to break its convictions. South of the line, Scotland began to settle into the pattern of the Presbyterianism we know to this day, and the sociology that made the Highland lairds into oppressors was eventually to ensure Presbyterianism took root in the north even more firmly than in the south.

## 75 Presbyterian and Episcopalian worship in 1700

The remarkable thing about Presbyterian and Episcopalian worship in 1700 is that despite all the tension of the previous 140 years and the fact that Episcopalians were for the most part regarded as unlawful, their services were practically the same. This surprised even contemporary observers. Thus Sir George MacKenzie in 1691:

> The Reader will be astonished, when we inform him: that the way of Worship in our Church differed nothing from what the Presbyterians themselves practised, (except only that we used the Doxologie, the Lord's Prayer, and in Baptism, the Creed, all which they rejected). We had no Ceremonies, Surplice, Altars, Cross in Baptisms, nor the meanest of things which would be allowed in England by the Dissenters, in way of Accommodation.

The same point was made by the author of 'The Case of the Present Afflicted Clergy in Scotland Truly Represented' (1690):

> The only difference is, our Clergy are not so overbold nor fulsome in their extemporary Expressions as the others are . . . and we generally conclude one of our prayers with that which our Saviour taught and commanded, which the other Party decry as Superstitious and Formal. Amen too gives great Offence, tho' neither the Clerk nor People use it, only the Minister sometimes shuts up his prayer with it. The Sacraments are Administered after the same Way and Manner by both: neither so much as kneeling at the Prayers, or when they receive the Elements of the Lord's Supper, but all sitting together at a long table in the Body of the Church or Chancel. In Baptism neither Party use the Cross, nor are any Godfathers or godmothers required, the Father only promising for his child.

Bishop Rattray, who died in 1720, was much less kind in his descriptions of how the congregations at that time vanished at great speed after the immensely lengthy and tedious service: and goes on to speak of how rarely they had the Eucharist. Here too, however, Presbyterians and Episcopalians were as one.

> They had their Preparation sermon (as they called it) the day before, their Action Sermon on the day itself, beside their discourses at the serving of the tables (for they had long tables placed in the church, on each side of which the people sat as if it had been at a common meal and handed about the Elements from one to another, whilst the attending elders shoved the plate with the consecrated Bread along the table for their greater conveniency, during which time a Presbyter was still discoursing to them). As for the consecration, that was performed by an extemporary Prayer, which how defective it must frequently have been may easily be judged considering that many of them had no notion of its being the Sacrifice of the Christian Church, only they repeated the words of the History of the Institution. And though they might proportion the Bread at first to the number of communicants before consecration: yet, at least in many places, they generally consecrated but a small part of the Wine, and when it was exhausted they add a little barrel or some other such vessel at hand, from which they filled more, and straight used it without any consecration at all.

There are two reactions to this. Thomas Morer, an English army chaplain in Scotland in 1690, is surprised that the two parties can still disagree! Bishop Rattray's attitude is a warning that their paths are now to part.

# V THE SHAPING OF THE KIRK OF TODAY

## SCHISM AND REUNION

### 76 Schisms and reunions: the story of a kirk divided

When the former Moderator of the General Assembly of the Church of Scotland is asked why Scotland's church history since the Reformation is a maze of divisions and reunions, he relishes giving the answer that it's because Scots care passionately about their religion! Be that as it may, the story is bewildering. The easiest place to begin this tale of divisions is with the settlement of Presbyterianism for Scotland by William of Orange in 1690. His fervent hope was unity and peace. In England this was relatively simple, with the minority Dissenters being allowed to exist alongside the established Episcopal church. In Scotland, he at first thought the same could apply but eventually decided to maintain Presbyterian government as fittest for government but to make it 'as supportable as possible to those who may dissent from it that they may fall in liking with it and so the kingdom might become one body'. The Episcopalians to this day maintain that they were robbed because of their Jacobite involvement and because there was an Assembly that was unrepresentative of the majority of Scotland. Presbyterians maintain that they represented the majority. This they did in Lowland Scotland but not in the north, and at that time the population was pretty evenly divided between north and south. Those placed in power were the ministers and lay people who were displaced in 1660 (the antedeluvians) but they hadn't nearly enough ministers to staff all the parishes. William's European experience had given him a distaste for persecution and so he made repeated efforts for Episcopalians to stay within the established church. In Anne's time this culminated in the 1712 Act which allowed Episcopalians who acknowledged Anne to worship outside the system. At this stage the Episcopal church as we know it became official (it already had some recognition from 1695 onwards). To this day all attempts at reunion have failed and the nature of the Episcopal church has changed over the years from being almost indistinguishable in doctrine and forms of worship from the Presbyterian church to now being sharply different in worship and arguably so also in doctrine.

Other divisions lie beneath the surface of this more or less permanent split. Many committed Covenanters like the Cameronians stayed outside the Presbyterian church and remained so for over a century or more depending on how their successors in the Covenanting tradition are defined (Dr Ian Paisley and Pastor Jack Glass look to them still). Within the emerging Episcopal church, division occurred immediately after the 1690 settlement between Non-Jurors, the great majority who stayed outside the system and resented the Church of England as much as the Presbyterians, and the Qualified, a smaller number who took the oath of loyalty to William and renunciation of James, modelling themselves on the Church of England and the Prayer Book there. The Qualified numbers grew as time went on and when the 1792 Act removed their penal disabilities it was on condition that the united groups conformed to the usages of the Church of England. The final shape of the Episcopal church became a reality in 1808, though Dr William Ferguson of the University of Edinburgh stresses that the real divide between the Episcopal church and the Presbyterian church took place in the nineteenth century, when Episcopalians accepted the tenets of the Oxford Movement and Presbyterians associated bishops with all they didn't want in a church.

## 77   Presbyterianism divided at its foundations

After William of Orange's settlement in 1690 a series of divisions arose from within the reformed kirk and raised questions as to whether Presbyterianism was doomed to breed endless divisions. The first pressure was a legacy of the past. As the parish system grew in the eleventh century, the parish churches were built thanks to landowner 'patrons' who retained certain rights with bishops as to the appointment of parish priests. These rights of patronage survived the *First Book of Discipline* despite all the authors' worries about Catholic patrons. The rights were reinforced by the fact that the parish had state duties devolved to it, particularly education and poor relief; but the problems of 'wrong' appointments caused the rights of patronage to come and go in the subsequent years, only to be firmly restored in 1712. This combined with the second internal pressure from the Enlightenment and the new ideas of the scientific age from Isaac Newton onwards. To define man as intended 'to worship God and enjoy Him for ever' and to accept Genesis and the miraculous seemed out of date to many and such 'enlightened' ministers being imposed by 'enlightened' patrons built resentment.

The first secession came in 1740 with Ebenezer Erskine of Stirling, his brother Ralph of Dunfermline and Wilson of Perth. Patronage was the main issue but also their desire to get away from the angry God of the Westminister Confession and portray a gracious God allowing his people to be brought into a real community of believers (Zwingli rather than Calvin). The next series of divisions centred on removing the principle of establishment and patronage altogether. Thomas Gillespie of Carnock built the Relief church on his links with the non-conformist churches in England. By the end of the eighteenth century, the Seceders, following the lead of the Relief, became Voluntaries, that is they argued for disestablishment.

Throughout the eighteenth and early nineteenth centuries,

tensions continued between the enlightenment ministers (Moderates) and the traditional 'evangelicals'; and between the church and state (Burghers and Anti-Burghers: New Light and Auld Licht; all Seceders). This tension increased with the new confidence in the middle class with the Reform Act of 1832: getting the political vote increased their conviction that they should be able to choose their ministers themselves. The evangelicals in the Church of Scotland managed to push through the Veto Act, which gave the congregation a veto over the patron's choice of minister, and the Chapel Act, which was designed to give chapel ministers full status. The idea was that the church should have extension by chapels-of-ease in places like Coatbridge where no kirk had existed before: but it was limited because chapel ministers didn't have the same status. The evangelicals under Thomas Chalmers were frustrated by the lack of any further progress. The government categorically refused to abolish patronage and so Chalmers in 1843 led about a third of the church from the Assembly at St Andrews and St George's in Edinburgh and marched with great crowds to the Tanfield Hall to establish the Free Church. Free from state interference, this church made light work of building churches throughout Scotland. Its evangelical zeal gave a tremendous impetus to Christian faith and led to renewal in the majority church left behind, but the cost was aptly called 'The Disruption'.

## 78   The painful way back to a united kirk

Disruption of the kirk was one thing but to put the pieces back
together again was a long slow process which has left a whole
range of small, still separate, Presbyterian churches in
Scotland. The church in Scotland has never until this century
been able to go its own way without state interference.
Achieving that has been the major achievement of the reunion
process but it took until 1929. The dynamism after the
Disruption of 1843 was quite incredible as the Free Church
with Chalmers, Cunningham, Candlish and Gordon built its
churches alongside the established ones (and even built New
College by 1846 with twenty people each contributing £1,000);
and the Church of Scotland recovered from the shock of being
abused as the 'residuary establishment' to regain vitality with
Professor Lee, Robert Lee of Greyfriars, Norman McLeod of
the Barony in Glasgow and John Tulloch of St Mary's College,
St Andrews. Basically it had the support of the upper and lower
classes while the Free Church drew its support from the middle
classes. Robert Lee, despite landing in hot water for it, brought
colour back into the church with stained glass, organ music and
liturgical movement; even the Free Church was influenced.

Despite the much divided state of Presbyterianism, the
tendency in the second half of the nineteenth century was
towards reunion. As early as 1847 the majority of the Seceders
and the majority of the Relief churches joined together to form
the United Presbyterian church, a large, influential and liberal
body. The next step came in the nineties when the Free Church
gave up the idea of persuading others that it should be the
established church and adopted the Voluntary principle. This
idea that the only way back to reunion and a revitalisation of the
church was freedom from the state grew on every side. Pressure
built up from the resentment of the Church of Scotland's role in
education and poor relief: the Voluntary churches felt
discriminated against and their poor were often sent back to

'their own church' without the help that was the only social welfare of the day. Until 1851 the Church of Scotland dominated the universities as every professor had to subscribe to their Confession of Faith. In 1874 Disraeli repealed the Act that had caused all the trouble, the Patronage Act, and so events began to move.

The feeling by the end of the nineteenth century was that the United Presbyterian church and the Free Church should merge. This caused its own difficulties. When the Free Church by a Declaratory Act of 1893 loosened its ties to the strict letter of the Westminster Confession, the Free Presbyterian Church was established in protest in the Highlands. Undeterred, the majority moved towards union. This was achieved in 1900 but the supporters of what is now known as the Free Church of Scotland stayed out. The next major challenge was the existence side by side of the United Free Church, Presbyterian, liberal and willing to look at the modern developments of science and not bound by the strict letter of the Westminster Confession, and the Church of Scotland which had moved largely in that direction. There were talks before 1914 but the union only finally took place in 1929: again a minority of the United Free Church remain to this day. The last possibility of state interference had now been removed and most Presbyterians were together again.

Scottish Churches' House, Dunblane

# EVANGELISM AND REVIVALISM

## 79 'Born again in Cambuslang'

Before the Reformation, popular religion in Scotland centred on the saints and this continued, despite the best efforts of the kirk, for at least decades afterwards. In the Highlands, a belief in charms, spells and fairies gave expression – fairly untroubled – to fears and hopes that could be described, too, as a form of popular religion. This 'white magic' was mirrored in darker vein by witchcraft to the extent that the seventeenth-century peasant is said to have known far more about the devil than about God.

In England, Methodism in the mid-eighteenth century embodied a very definite popular religion but Wesley, despite a series of visits to Scotland between 1740 and 1790, failed to repeat his success and decided you 'can't teach the Scots anything'. Methodism in Scotland became established in small ways both then and again in the nineteenth century but never caught the popular imagination. It did, however, have a role in the beginnings of the religious revival movement which burst out now and then throughout the seventeenth century and gave a folk basis for the revivalism of the nineteenth century.

The first and most famous of these revivals took place in Cambuslang, just outside Glasgow, in 1742 and its fame spread not just throughout Scotland but also through England, the Netherlands and America (where Scots settlers had had a similar revival in 1730). Within two months crowds of more than 20,000 gathered to hear the famous English evangelist George Whitefield. The Cambuslang Wark, as it was called, was catalogued by the local minister William McCulloch. Of the one hundred testimonies – 'I was made to see . . . that I must be born again' – seventy-five were women and most were in their twenties. Neither kirk nor landlords were amused: eviction was the penalty for many literate but very much working-class supporters and this served to feed an already clear antipathy between them and the landlords. John Napier, at the age of twenty-one, is typical of the young people who resisted:

> Next day the gentle Man in whose ground I lived sent his Officer for me and another lad . . . . and he discharged us not to go to Cambuslang, threatning that if we did he would arreist our crop and turn us out of his land: for that he was informed that when we came home we could not work any next day, and he particularly abused a certain minister George Whitefield with his tongue calling him a Mountebank and a Damn'd rascal, who was putting all the people mad. He added that if we could read our catechism we needed no more religion: and that if we would stay more at home at our work and go less to Cambuslang to hear that Damd's rascal and get our brains crack'd we might pay our rent better and work better.

Definite echoes of the charismatic movement today are in the testimonies: thus the three-hour dialogue between McCulloch and a certain Catherine Jackson.

> To each of her many hysterical outbursts, McCulloch responded with some promise from the Scripture. 'Come', said the Minister, 'Shall we pray for a Pull of God's almight arm to draw you to Christ?' 'O yes, yes', said She, and got up on her feet. At this time there was a great Stir . . . the joys of some were plainly transporting and almost too strong for them to contain . . . and there was a sound of weeping among others, that might be heard at a considerable distance.

Cambuslang had made its mark.

## 80 'The Men'

All eyes in the room settle on 'The Man' – an austere, quasi-mystical, long-haired character wearing a long, blue cloak and a spotted handkerchief around his head. A ripple of anticipation runs through the Friday 'Question Meeting' at the Highland Communion weekend or the 'ordinary congregational meeting' or even in some places at the Family Sabbath Evening Fellowship Meeting. This is why small groups or major meetings of up to 1,000 (as at Durness in the mid-nineteenth century) gathered from throughout the Highlands – to listen to 'The Men', the caste of lay evangelising zealots, as they expounded who had the marks to allow them to go to communion. They exist to this day but were especially common in parts of the Highland and Islands from 1760 to 1850.

There are all sorts of theories as to the origins of 'The Men': is there a follow-through in Highland culture of the old Celtic bards or even the Druid and the 'magus', or is there a spontaneous lay leadership built on St Paul's ideals of the Christian community and the Scottish distrust of any too great a place to be given to the minister, especially if that minister was the imposition of a lay patron with Episcopal leanings? Whatever the theory, however, we can see some of the formative elements in their development towards holding an important place in Highland society. They set such extreme standards of behaviour that only a fraction of the congregations were deemed worthy to partake of communion. Card-playing, dancing, even using an umbrella could all lead to deep trouble! The earliest memories centre on John Munro, the celebrated 'caird of Kiltearn'. He was a disciple of Thomas Hogg and this brings 'The Men' very firmly into the evangelical, Presbyterian and Calvinist Free Church tradition because he was ejected at the Restoration, restored at the Revolution and died there in 1692. Hogg was much impressed by student praying societies in Aberdeen and linked them in Kiltearn with the tradition of private house meetings away from the ministers (which are attested to by an unsigned letter from Dundee dated as early as 8 January 1651). He trained Munro and from his inspiration there developed a group who, while very individual in what they did, were marked by a strong sense of brotherhood with one another and an incredibly retentive use of the Bible balanced by a prayer life. Of Hugh Mann of Creich it was said 'whether walking on the high road or working in the fields, he was continually engaged in prayer and almost always in an audible voice'. William Fraser 'prayed for more than an hour. But such a prayer! Another hour of it would have been no burden to either a Christian or a poet'. When the Synod of Caithness and Sutherland tried in 1737 to suppress the meetings at which 'The Men' had become publicly attractive figures, they resisted for twenty years and won. This undoubtedly made God visible in those remote communities and promoted the stubborn independence that Secession and Free Church alike built on to preserve what they saw as essential values. Sadly, however, 'the common frailties and infirmities of believers evoked neither their sympathy or their forgiveness' and their role in preparing for communion was such that 'they surrounded it with such formidable and insufficient hedges as made it an almost empty table'. To this day, however, their successors in the Highlands and Islands provide the mainstay of the Friday Fellowship Meeting, and give austere witness to one form of Christian faith.

## 81  Changes in Episcopalian and Catholic worship

Despite the apparently separate paths taken by the Presbyterian churches, the Episcopal church and the Roman Catholic church in the past 300 years, changes in both Episcopal and Catholic churches came to be important not only within these churches but even as a stimulus to worship in the Presbyterian churches. The story begins in 1690 with the split in Episcopalians between the Non-Jurors, the majority who refused to accept William and were pronounced illegal, and the Qualified who accepted him and the Church of England Prayer Book. There had been no real difference between Episcopal and Presbyterian worship up to this point but in the period between the split and the coming together of the branches of the Episcopal church in 1792 and 1808, an attractive and distinctively Scottish worship developed. They attacked the Presbyterians for 'strident and incoherent harangues'. Scholars looked back to the 1552 Prayer Book of Edward VI and some to that of 1549 but some mixed in extempore prayers in the Presbyterian fashion. The Lord's Prayer, the creed and doxology had always had an honoured place but other elements came in from the closer connection with Church of England ritual. It was only, however, from 1860 onwards that the onlooker would find a radically different worship in Scottish Episcopal churches as well as a clearer vision of bishops as the 'divinely ordained form of church government'. Under the leadership of the bishop of Brechin, the Anglo-Catholic Tractarian movement brought the sort of ritual – beautiful music and even candles and incense – that the present Episcopal bishop of Edinburgh, Richard Holloway, looks back to as the elements which brought him as a teenager from Presbyterian worship to the Episcopal church.

Roman Catholic worship after the Reformation was quite different from the solemn musical ceremonies of medieval times which had been a matter of the mass read quietly in Latin by itinerant priests on a temporary altar stone. Presbyterian worship was of course austere, with psalms led by precentors the only variety on the minister's spoken word right up to the end of the nineteenth century. In 1789 one or two priests tried to introduce hymns to Catholic worship, giving rise to the popular story that they were the source of the errand boys of Edinburgh starting whistling *Adeste Fideles* as they did their work. Both the Highland church in Aberdeen in 1789 and a Benedictine monk in 1793 in Dunfermline were told to stop hymn singing for fear of upsetting the Presbyterians. Confidence grew, however. Aberdeen had the first post-Reformation high mass in 1804 and Edinburgh Cathedral installed the first organ in 1814. We find a priest in the north composing a book of church music and the seminary at Aquhorties producing a modest hymn book. The standards of church music grew and even tiny churches had organs and choirs. This produced the strange phenomenon of Presbyterians queueing to pay to hear the music. In Aberdeen, an oratorio raised money for a Fever Hospital; in Glasgow, money was collected for schools. The revolution of music in Catholic churches prompted change in Presbyterian worship in much the same way that the sweeping worship changes in the Catholic church of the 1960s – with modern English and congregational participation – have stimulated changes of worship in the Church of Scotland today.

## 82   Heresy on trial

Tension built up during the 1987 Assembly of the Free Church of Scotland with moves behind the scenes for a heresy trial against some of the leading professors in the church. It reminded many of the passions of the nineteenth century concerning the Westminster Confession of Faith.

In the 1830s a number of heresy trials arose from attempts to present God with a more loving image, a God who offered salvation to all and who didn't predestine some to heaven and some to hell. The person of Christ too was refilled with His humanity and this was seen as undermining His divinity. Thus the trials of John McLeod Campbell and Edward Irving. It was 'enlightened thought' versus traditional Calvinism.

Social reform was the next source of tension. In the forties, Chalmers believed that making people better would solve social problems. Others like the Reverend Patrick Brewster of Paisley Abbey got into trouble with Glasgow Presbytery for speaking at Chartist rallies in the belief that social reform alone could clear the way to allow people to be better. Then again worship was generally recognised as boring but the attempts of Robert Lee at Greyfriars to introduce colour and an organ into the rebuilt church with kneeling for prayer in church meant that he was arraigned to appear before the Assembly to meet accusations of unsettling church order. He died before the trial and his ideas were in the main to triumph.

In the central area of what Christians should believe, this sort of triumph of the persecuted also took place. The most important example was a man regarded by many as the greatest home-based theologian Scotland ever produced. William Robertson Smith was professor of Old Testament in the Free Church College in Aberdeen. His reputation for the balanced understanding of the importance of literary forms in understanding the Bible led him to be invited to contribute an article to the *Encyclopaedia Britannica* of 1875. The fundamentalists were horrified that he should question Moses' authorship of the first five books of the Bible and other similar issues. The trials continued for six years until in 1880 he was reprieved from the threat of being sacked. His supporters had no sooner celebrated his triumph, however, when he wrote another article in 1881 and was deposed. Principal Rainy of New College failed to save him but managed to prevent his views from being condemned and so they were still taught. A group of distinguished scholars including T.M. Lindsay issued a declaration of support the following day and said 'Come and get us'. Nobody did. Victory had been snatched from the teeth of defeat. Robertson Smith went to Cambridge and died a young man but his reputation was international and his influence in Scotland was such that all that he had taught now became quietly the standard approach. The UP church in 1879, the Free Church in 1892 and the Auld Kirk at the turn of the century all officially recognised that the Westminster Confession need not be adhered to literally. Was it all progress? Dr William Ferguson of the University of Edinburgh likes to issue a warning note: a church without a creed is a somewhat peculiar institution. Is this a reason for empty kirks today?

## 83　The new Revivalism and the new Gothic revival

Revival or the like was the name of the game for the kirk in the nineteenth century, despite the divisions which ripped it apart. The revival, however, took quite different forms. Worship had become desperately dull. It continued for two hours and was practically a one-man-band effort by the minister. The structure was Psalm – Extempore Prayer – Scripture with running commentary – Psalm – Sermon – Extempore Prayer – Psalm. It was acceptable in Covenanting days when the minister was fired up with zeal but in quieter times it was boring. Some went back to Knox for a fuller liturgy. Others went in what could be called a Scoto-Catholic direction. They felt that a church should look like a church, in other words that it should be built in the Gothic style. Thus there was a chancel, a side pulpit and a communion table that looked like an altar. There was also the return of prayers of sorrow, the Lord's Prayer and communion services.

The second approach to renewal was quite different for it was a revival of popular preaching. Here the church – as in the old St George's West in Edinburgh – became a preaching theatre.

Dr Andrew Ross of New College sees a major loss in both revivals, because the first post-Reformation kirks had no seats and for communion long tables were brought in which allowed a hundred at a time to come forward and sit down at the table for communion – a much better symbol of the Lord's Supper. Currie Kirk was built for this: the long table would have been in the long section of the T shape. The lack of emphasis on communion in both revivals was unfaithful to Calvin's tradition. The idea in the Free Church today that perhaps two out of a hundred go to communion is again foreign to his thought. Dr Ross believes it is close to making communion a reward for achievement – the heresy of works.

The final approach to revival came from the American scene

and consisted in the amazing conversion campaigns of Moody and Sankey. Moody was a Chicago salesman who was converted by a Revivalist preacher and worked first in the YMCA and then as an unordained preacher. He combined with Sankey who used the popular music-hall style of the day to attract people to their services. They took over, for example, the massive engine sheds of the Union Pacific Railroad in Philadelphia and thousands packed their meetings. The services were sentimental at times but relevant and lively, though the more staid members of Edinburgh and Glasgow congregations found them shocking or at least lacking in due dignity and decorum. Moody and Sankey are regarded as the Billy Grahams of the 1870s, working only with the consent of the local churches on the basis that their instant conversion had to lead to a secure base in a local church community. Most converts seemed to have been from the middle classes. The douce, middle-of-the-road people went in large numbers to the open-air rallies that in a sense amounted to the last radical new departure in the development of the spread of the Christian message in Scotland. Until then Christianity was always seen as something to be steadily nurtured over the years in the day-to-day life of parish and local kirk. In the face of the churchless masses, a new way had been found to be effective and it has been repeated in different forms ever since.

## 84 Missions abroad

The idea of Scots going abroad to spread the message of the Christian faith began rather paradoxically with the remarkable Haldane family revival in the 1790s which led them to be concerned about mission in the Highlands. From their independent chapels came not only the present-day Baptists and Congregationalists, but also a concern for non-Christians which flatly contradicted the strangely Calvinist view (in the Seceders) that it was arrogant to try to do God's work of calling people to the church.

It was only in the late eighteenth century that the Church of Scotland in all its divided parts got round to missions. Before that, all the great characters emerged from the independent chapels with the London Missionary Society co-ordinating their efforts. Thus Livingstone, Moffat and Philip.

David Livingstone emerged from a chapel in Wishaw but has his religious roots in the Gaelic culture of Lismore. He was a brilliant linguist and skilled at getting along with the blacks and becoming their friend. A group of Africans even walked with him on his journeys. He didn't directly convert many but opened the doors for others. In political terms, his record was ahead of his time. For fourteen years in South Africa, he made it clear that blacks should get civil rights. In Botswana, he said, 'Everyone knows where I stand in the clash between black and white.' He even acquired guns for his people to defend themselves against the Boers.

Robert Moffat came from a chapel in the north-east and became a father-figure in his long missionary life in Botswana and in his courageous friendship with the war-like Matabele Zulus in Zimbabwe. John Philip came from a Congregationalist chapel in Aberdeen and was perhaps the central figure of all, both for mission work in South Africa and for the political struggle on behalf of the black population. The first Scots missionaries in Blantyre in Malawi, David Scott and Alex

Hetherwick, engaged in a critique over many years of Britain's role in Nyasaland, speaking up for the blacks without fear or favour and active in the campaign against slavery, both in Africa and in America (here in Scotland, there were fierce arguments against accepting money from American Presbyterian churches on the basis that they were slave-owners). Scotland then can be proud of the Independent tradition, which on the one hand didn't neglect social justice in its zeal to spread the gospel and on the other hand inspired the Church of Scotland itself to take up the missionary outreach that in 'Faithshare' is still enriching the kirk on a two-way basis.

Dr Andrew Ross of New College observes that many went to Africa because of frustration with the kirk in Scotland. He tells the story of Willie Scott (brother of the David Scott who built the famous Blantyre church), who ran a boys' club in the Cowgate while studying as a medical and theological student. When leaving for Africa, he told them at the club that he was sure that if Christ came to Edinburgh, he would teach not in St Giles or in Free St George's but in the Cowgate. Such realistic idealism was perhaps the strength of the Scottish Missionary Movement and its lesson for today. Neither this aspect nor the courageous championing of the rights of black people at a time when it was far from fashionable have been given proper credit in the telling of their story.

# HIGHLANDS AND CITIES

## 85  The evangelism of the Highlands

The Highlands remained mostly Catholic for a long time after the Reformation and then were Episcopalian after that. The nineteenth century saw the whole character of religious life there changed by an evangelistic outreach that came mainly from the dissenting branches of the Presbyterian church. It began with the Secessionist churches of Ebenezer Erskine and the Relief churches of Thomas Gillespie. The first toe-hold was in Argyll and Kintyre with two congregations at Campbeltown and Southend. The next thrust came from Robert and James Haldane (Gleneagles; Airthrie Castle, now in Stirling University; and Edinburgh) who began in the Established church but soon branched out with the 'Society for Propagating the Gospel at Home': missionaries journeyed far and near throughout the Highlands from Lewis and Tiree right through to Aberdeenshire. The movement is important not only because of the change in the Highlands and the way that was opened for Free Church popularity after the Disruption of 1843 but also because of the two Christian denominations who still contribute to church life today.

The first strand is the Congregational Church which has close links with the ideals of the French revolution through Robert Haldane: it sets the local congregation as the decision-making body above both the elders and the wider church. Some Congregationalists came to Scotland with Cromwell and some, such as Lady Glenorchy's Church in Edinburgh, began within the Established church. The real beginning of Scottish Congregationalism is, however, the establishment of 'Tabernacles' (under the influence of John Whitfield) by the Haldane brothers beginning with the Circus church (an old theatre) at the head of Leith Walk in Edinburgh. They were particularly strong along the East Coast right up to Orkney and Shetland. Greville Ewing, minister of Lenorchy Church, had the distinction of forming the actual Congregationalist Union.

The second strand came when the Haldanes – because of their interest in the New Testament and a 'gathered church' of adult believers making their profession of faith – became Baptists in 1808. In places like Aberdeen there had been a few Baptists left after Cromwell's invasion and then a new beginning called Scotch Baptists from 1760 onwards who owed much to John Glass of Tealing in Angus and his 'spiritual church' which was not 'of this world'. Archibald McLean and Robert Campbell are names to note here in Edinburgh and Glasgow. The Haldane preachers brought a new wave of more outward-looking Baptists such as William Carey who went to India and provided the inspiration for men like Christopher Anderson, the founder of Charlotte Baptist Chapel in Edinburgh. They are known as English Baptists. Christopher Anderson was again a pioneer evangelist in the Highlands and founded the Gaelic school society in 1810. The English Baptists (who didn't really owe anything to England) came to dominate over the Scotch Baptists (who had a plurality of pastors as opposed to the one pastor with deacons) but were always a minority church in Scotland. Angus McLean estimates that there were four or five hundred in the 1780s and 5,000 by 1841 with 1,000 of these being Gaelic speaking.

Stirring times then in the Highlands; a great many church splits and a great deal of effective evangelism.

## 86   The Catholic mission in the Highlands

The studies of Fr Mark Dilworth and the Very Reverend Dr Duncan Shaw in recent years have highlighted how much of the Highlands stayed Catholic or were neglected after the Reformation – and here we're talking about two-thirds of the area of Scotland and where 50 per cent of the population spoke Gaelic. By the end of the eighteenth century, there were only a few Catholics in most areas of Scotland but the West Highlands still had strong Catholic communities. Much of this was due to the Irish Gaelic-speaking missionaries, who from 1619 onwards came across the sea (the easiest means of communication at that time for the whole of the west coast) from places like a Franciscan friary in Antrim. Cornelius Ward, for example, made the most of being a fully trained Gaelic bard to approach the chiefs and travel around celebrating mass. Vincentians, Dominicans, Jesuits and secular priests all played their part in a haphazard mission that was paralleled by haphazard harassment. It was a dangerous life, as was shown when Fr Robin Munro, ill and with a high fever, was thrown into a dungeon at Glengarry Castle, where he subsequently died.

The first post-Reformation Catholic Vicar-Apostolic (Bishop), Thomas Nicholson, was appointed in 1694. In 1697 he arrived in Scotland and a three-year journey throughout Scotland brought the beginnings of church organisation.

The missionary outreach of the Presbyterian churches in the eighteenth and nineteenth centuries brought clear divisions between unchurched areas which had now become strongly Protestant and traditional Catholic areas such as Barra, South Uist, Eriskay, Morar, Arisaig and Lochaber in the West Highlands; Strathglass, Banff and Aberdeenshire in the East Highlands and Glenlivet in the north. In the 1690s and then after the 1715 and 1745 rebellions there was immense harassment of Catholics but it didn't last too long and the communities survived. After the '45, all the Catholic chapels were burned and the priests put on the run or imprisoned in prison hulks off England where some of them died. Yet within ten years, all the chapels were rebuilt and much improved.

In 1727, Rome divided Scotland by language into a Highland District and a Lowland District: George Hay is typical of a line of impressive bishops who were appointed. He was an Episcopalian medical student who accompanied the Jacobite army tending the wounded during the '45. Imprisoned in London, he became a Catholic, then studied in Rome and returned to Scotland as a priest, subsequently becoming bishop. His policy was that Catholics should quite literally live down their reputations as Jacobites, and this, with the help of reaction to the French Revolution, they managed to do by the end of the century. The government saw them as the victims of a common enemy and even helped with seminaries in Scalan, Lismore and Aquhorties. The next crisis was the Highland Clearances which devastated the Catholic Highlands. Most people went to Canada but some settled in Glasgow and Edinburgh. In the 1790s, David Dale of New Lanark fame – a Protestant himself – founded a chapel in Glasgow for those who came to work in the cotton industry. By then, Irish immigration was beginning and that would switch the focus of Catholic life from the Highlands to the cities.

## 87   Free Kirk and Highlands

From 1711 to 1815 we have what Dr William Ferguson of the University of Edinburgh describes as an unseen revolution in the Highlands from a population totally inimical to Presbyterianism to a population devoted to it. The breakdown in the social order – ending feudalism and encouraging individual self-determination – which gave Presbyterianism its triumph in the Lowlands arrived later in the Highlands and so Episcopalianism dominated right up to that point. The chiefs and lairds were Episcopalian: the people followed suit. Once the clan system broke down, people became free to make their own decisions. The chief became a landlord and therefore an oppressor, with the clearances bringing that conflict and that identification to a tragic climax. The clearances were seen as an Old Testament punishment from God and, as the people recoiled from the religion of their oppressing landlords, they turned to the Calvinist stress on everyone finding their own way to God. It was a movement of individual conscience rather than democracy and so was a rich seedbed for the new-found evangelism of the kirk in the early eighteenth century. This is the parallel influence to Thomas Chalmers' evangelical call in the cities and many of the ministers were trained by him. Self-help and an individual response to the Lord came together with the call to be free from the patronage of the great landowners in the appointment of their ministers. As a result, the domination of the kirk's Assemblies in the forties by the evangelicals came from the new upsurge in the Highlands (and the 'Parliamentary kirks' built as extensions at that time to the parish ministry) and when the Disruption came in 1843, the Highlands became almost totally Free Church. In Aberdeen, every single minister went over to the Free Church and in the glens it was almost as much of a clean sweep. The push for church extension before the Disruption and the burning enthusiasm of the Free Church afterwards led to kirks being built right through the Highlands. This was made possible by the wide support for the Free Church in the middle classes and the fund that Chalmers had organised with such brilliant efficiency whereby the wealthier areas set aside money to support the poor parishes in the Highlands.

The fact that it was the Free Church tradition that evangelised the Highlands in this way in the nineteenth century had other effects. Professor A.C. Cheyne, now retired from the University of Edinburgh, stresses the fact that the Free Church – as with most reforms – had as its motto 'Ask for the old paths and walk in them'. It looked to Knox, Melville and the Covenanters and began with an austere sermon-centred worship. As the century went on, the Highland churches – because of their remoteness – were less affected by the liberalising changes in worship and in attitudes to science and the Westminster Confession of Faith that were to lead to the breaking away of first the Free Presbyterian church and then the Free Church of Scotland as we now know it today. They stayed outside the reunions convinced that the Free Church had deserted its principles and was forgetting its ideals. Their strength to this day remains in the Highlands and Islands and has shaped the identikit that we all recognise as Highland Christian faith.

## 88   Chalmers: the gospel should set us free

Thomas Chalmers was born in 1780 and brought up in a strict
Calvinist home before going to St Andrews University at the
age of twelve. In 1803, he became minister at Kilmany in Fife.
His real interests were mathematics and science until serious
illness in 1811 brought him an evangelical conversion which
turned him into a charismatic preacher capable of thrilling
congregations and generations of student ministers alike. The
year 1815 saw him confronting urban poverty in the Tron Kirk
in Glasgow and persuading the city to open a new parish for him
to cater for the vast numbers of unchurched poor. In Kilmany,
the kirk's statutory care for the widows and the poor worked
because everything was on a small scale and so Chalmers
divided St John's parish into twenty units (in Mary Furgol's
classic description 'Billy Connolly-type tenement close'). Each
would have a deacon and would be responsible for the poor
relief in the unit. Chalmers believed that this plan would
eliminate poverty but his judgment was clouded by his own
view that the preaching of the gospel and the individual's
response to it would allow the person to rise above his poverty.
As Professor A.C. Cheyne, former Principal of New College,
puts it: 'Chalmers believed the poor were pauperised by handouts.' Recent research has shown that though Chalmers
achieved an immense amount by putting poverty on the agenda
of all the churches, his own practical plans didn't work. Fewer
and fewer people approached the deacons for help because of
the inquisition that they had to face and the implicit stigma that
was involved. He only stayed in St John's for four years and one
of his successors, McGill, came to believe that Andrew
Thomson of the University of Edinburgh was right when he
declared that only the government could change the situation.
Social justice should precede the preaching of salvation in a
future life. Debate with an Episcopalian, William Allison,
failed to convince Chalmers that the gospel would only set men

free when it was used first to put bread in men's stomachs . His popularity, however, placed poverty on everyone's agenda once and for all.

The war against poverty, however, was only one aspect of Chalmers' work. His incisive preaching and brilliant organisation led to extension churches being built to bring the gospel message throughout Scotland. He became convinced that the kirk would never reach the unchurched unless it broke free from the frustrations of state control. He led the Free Church out into the Disruption with a sad heart but a burning conviction that this was the only way to enable the state to do what it should, namely reinforce the church rather than limit and control it. Before and after the Disruption, his brilliant teaching (the students stood and cheered his lectures!) inspired a whole generation of ministers for the kirk. He raised the money for the Free Kirk out of nothing and financed expansion in such a way that the rich kirks helped to pay for poor parishes in remote parts of the Highlands and Islands. Perhaps his best epitaph is that when he began his work the status of minister was at its lowest ever: by the time he died, he had raised its status in a way that has lasted until today. Both the Free Church of Scotland and the Church of Scotland revere his intellectual achievements, continue to reflect on his challenges about the poor and the unchurched, and are inspired by the perseverance and brilliance of both his preaching and his organisation. The two are still rarely found together.

## 89   The Catholic mission in the cities

The first Catholic church after the Reformation that could be
described as a real church was built in 1780 at Presholme in the
Enzie. In the cities mass was still being offered in private houses
but changes were afoot. In 1800 Edinburgh had two chapels in
Blackfriars Wynd, one for the Gaelic community and one for
the bishop: Bishop Geddes used to walk to Glasgow and back to
say mass. Dundee and Aberdeen too had little house chapels.
Glasgow had the little chapel made possible by the generosity of
David Dale of New Lanark as part of his social concern. Then
Irish immigration into the cities transformed the whole
situation and faced the Catholic church with a massive
missionary problem. In 1817 the present cathedral was built in
Glasgow with Gillespie Graham as the architect and Bishop
Andrew Scott devising a penny a week scheme to tackle the
enormous debt, a scheme which worked at first but failed when
unemployment grew. After the Irish famine in the forties, the
Catholic population had leapt to 100,000 and by 1914 there
were half a million in Glasgow and the West of Scotland alone.
The challenge was enormous for it wasn't just a spiritual one
but also what's known as the problem of urbanisation, the vast
range of difficulties that come about when a people who have
been used to the country have now to get used to city life. It's a
problem that has its echoes right through the Third World
today.

To meet spiritual needs, the Catholic church recruited
priests from Ireland (1,600 served from the famine until the
1920s) and also from Belgium, Germany and the Netherlands.
Michael Condon is a good example of the best of a whole
generation of such priests. At great personal cost, he was self-
educated in Ireland and then in 1846 came to Scotland, where
he quite literally slaved himself for the poor in the Greenock
and Gourock areas for over fifty years. The image of priests in
Scotland had been dramatically improved by French

Revolution priest exiles working in the schools teaching French, and by men like Charles Gordon in Aberdeen who fearlessly visited the cholera wards when ministers refused to do so. Priests in those days seemed either to have died young from such generosity or to have lived to a remarkably ripe old age! Irish priests like Michael Condon added to the church's respectability not only by their dedicated selflessness for the poor (in contrast with the Protestant work ethic which still suggested that if you were poor it was because you didn't try hard enough), but also by a passionate interest in and study of things Scottish. It was not only poverty that bound the Catholic community together, but also the resentment it experienced as an immigrant community alternately exploited as cheap labour doing the jobs no one else would do or seen as a threat to employment when times were hard. Like the American black community, it raised its own professional class of doctors and teachers, but this at the cost of great sacrifice in the rest of the family. In addition, Catholic revivalist techniques were used to great effect (working on hellfire and damnation balanced by emotional piety), with great stress on the sacraments of the Eucharist and Confession: the result was a strong but clerically-dominated community. The St Vincent de Paul Society – the pennies of the poor looking after the poor – stood out, however, as a lay-run service of social welfare for every conceivable need. Social and football clubs grew from a vision of caring that we could do with today.

## CHURCH AND POLITICS

### 90   A Jacobite church: the danger of church-state alignment

Right from the time of Columba, the Scottish church had been up to its neck in politics. St Columba was a 'political animal' as we would now term it, for his close relationship with the Scots kings of Dalriada and his careful negotiation with the king of the Picts gave Christianity a platform on which to build. From then on, kings saw themselves as having a responsibility to work for the good of the church and a grateful church tended to work for the security of the kingdom. The phenomenon of the Jacobite church in the eighteenth century illustrates only too clearly the danger the Christian church faces in every age, the danger of being too closely identified with one political party or viewpoint. The French and Russian revolutions illustrate the point in a more dramatic fashion – and South and Central American politics today give a more current lesson – but the Jacobite church has its own stark lessons on the Scottish scene.

Many who think of the Jacobite movement think of it as a Catholic movement against which William of Orange (Battle of the Boyne and all that) triumphed. In fact there were very few Catholics in Scotland at that time and they lived in remote parts such as Banffshire and the Outer Isles. When the Reverend Alexander Webster analysed the population in 1755, only a tiny proportion, 16,000-17,000, were Catholics. Catholics would be Jacobites of course because James VII had given them freedom from the penal laws – William of Orange, on the other hand, tightened the laws against Catholics to a severity greater than ever; they couldn't even own their own property – but the main body of Jacobite strength was Episcopalian. Episcopalians then had much the same worship and doctrine as the Presbyterians but differed as to how the church should be governed. In this regard, they saw James as the only hope for their form of church government, even though bishops had been coming and going in the post-Reformation years with the political wind of the day. When William came to Scotland, the Episcopal bishops made it impossible for him to recognise them by refusing him the oath of loyalty and continuing to swear allegiance to James whom they had regarded, in the light of the 'divine right of kings', as having been unjustly deposed. The fact that some bishops 'qualified' themselves was not enough to prevent their political Jacobitism taking them from their seemingly secure place in running the local churches to being outcasts having to find new churches and meeting-places with little money to do so and with the ever-present threat of persecution. Even the Covenanters had as their main objection to bishops the fact that they had been imposed by the crown in 1660. Loyalty to that crown brought imprisonment for some in 1689 and ejection for the rest to a life of poverty. After the Jacobite rebellion in 1715, as many as thirty of the ministers were proceeded against in the Edinburgh area alone. The size of a tolerated congregation was reduced from nine to four: and it was only by 1760 that George III could see Episcopal clergy as less of a threat. In 1788, Bonnie Prince Charlie's death left a Roman Catholic cardinal as the only 'pretender', so Episcopalians finally came to terms with the situation. In 1792, the penal laws against them were repealed but Jacobitism had reduced the Episcopal Protestant church from the centre stage to a minority status. The warning is valid for all Christian identification with the state.

## 91   Lay patronage and popular protest

Scottish history is marked by popular protest of one kind or another, even right up to the present day. So too is the story of Scottish Christian religion. Well known are the riots of the Reformation; the St Giles' Day riot of 1558 and the 'rascal multitude' of Perth (which had an anticlerical tradition anyway) who tore down the friaries and the Carthusian priory of the Charterhouse after hearing John Knox preach on 11 May 1559. In point of fact there were few riots and they were just as likely to be Catholic riots of protest, as in Kirkwall in February 1561 after a Protestant service was imposed and in Edinburgh in 1565 when a Catholic priest was manhandled after his trial. Later there was the famous St Giles' riot of 1637 which was attributed (wrongly, as it happens) to the name of Jenny Geddes. After 1780, the riot or demonstration became a vehicle of political opposition. There were meal mobs, protests against toll bars, militia riots, weavers' strikes and King's Birthday riots in 1792 and 1796. Despite there being intense feeling against both Catholics and Protestant dissenters, 1778 was the date of the last major anti-popery riot, and in 1792, when the Lord Advocate tried to raise a mob against the Unitarian meeting-place it instead turned into the King's Birthday riot.

On one issue, however, political and religious disagreements did combine to produce a riot – and that was the imposition of ministers by lay patrons on Presbyterian parishes. The right to do this had been restored as far back as 1712 (and only finally disappeared in 1874) but on at least twenty occasions between 1780 and 1815 alone, a minister was forcibly imposed on a parish. One amusing example is shown in Galt's *Annals of the Parish* in the person of the Reverend Mr Balwhidder who relates his experiences:

> We all got to the kirk door, it was found to be nailed up, so as by no possibility to be opened. The sergeant of the soldiers wanted

to break it, but I was afraid that the heritors would grudge and complain of the expense of a new door, and I supplicated him to let it be as it was: we were, therefore, obligated to go in by a window, and the crowd followed us in the most irreverent manner, making the Lord's house like an win on a fair day, with their grievious yellyhooing. During the time of the psalm and sermon, they behaved themselves better, but when the induction came on, their clamor was dreadful and Thomas Thoul, the weaver, a pious zealot in that time, he got up and protested and said, 'Verily, verily, I say unto you, he that entereth not by the door into the sheepfold, but climbeth up some other way, the same is a thief and a robber.'

At other times, there was sustained and hostile resistance. At Newburgh in Fife in 1785, we read how the incumbent, Dr Greenlow, found his pulpit 'laid thick with human excrement', the bell rope removed, the mysterious reappearance of the bell when it was noisily rung during his sermon, the shuttering of the windows so he couldn't see to read and the congregation 'repeatedly huzzaing in the church, in a most indecent and profane manner and by striking and beating with sticks or with their feet and hands upon the seats of the church'. It sounds very much like a modern political meeting and some of it makes today's popular protests seem pretty tame indeed.

## 92   Catholic Emancipation

At the Reformation, Catholics were quite simply not allowed to
exist. The way back was long and weary. Bernard Aspinwall of
the University of Glasgow has a telling summary. 'In a sense
Catholics got legal rights in 1829, in 1918 effective political
rights and in 1945 true social rights.' The French Revolution
brought Catholics sympathy and eventually the basic legal and
political rights of 1829; the First World War destroyed the class
system and the Second World War underlined the horrors of
treating any group of people as the Jews were treated. Because
of the bitterness of the Covenanting years, Scotland had to
change quite a bit before tolerance could be established. In
England, a Relief Act of 1778 allowed Catholics to exist but
there were immediate riots in Scotland which prevented a
parallel bill the following year. Bishop Hay (himself a
remarkable character) returned to Edinburgh to find a mob
burning his library and had to take refuge in Edinburgh Castle.
That night three different houses were attacked in Edinburgh
with parallel activity in Glasgow and Perth right up to 1793. It's
well known now that Catholic Emancipation came about in
England because of the political pressure of Daniel O'Connell
and the Irish situation. Despite the riots and rabble-rousing,
Protestant members of the Liberal party saw the move as the
logical result of their ideals and were delighted. What's not so
well known is that the Church of Scotland almost achieved
Catholic Emancipation without any help from Ireland. What
happened was that a quite remarkable character, Sir John
Joseph Dillon, a Knight of the Holy Roman Empire, addressed
the General Assembly in 1812 and persuaded them to pass a
motion supporting emancipation, a position remarkably at odds
with some of the anti-Catholic pronouncements when John
Cormack raised the banner of sectarianism a century later. The
House of Commons almost accepted the kirk's overture until
the move was denounced by Bishop Milner, a Roman Catholic

conservative bishop in England. So Scotland had to wait for the Irish.

Once people were legally allowed to become Catholics, nineteenth-century Scotland saw a series of prominent converts. Two of these are intriguing. The first was Sir William Drummond Stuart from a castle in Perthshire, who was at Waterloo and in the Peninsular War before going to the Wild West with the artist Alfred Jacob Miller. Taken ill among the trappers, he became a Catholic and so when he returned to take over his estate, he became – as well as the author of two novels about the Wild West – a major benefactor of churches in Edinburgh and Dundee. The second was Robert Monteith, who succeeded to his father's textile fortune in 1848 but not before a distinguished academic career at Glasgow and Cambridge; his friends included Thackeray, Tennyson and a lord who owned the greatest collection of pornography of the time. He married Wilhelmina Mellish, daughter of the man who translated Schiller's *Mary Queen of Scots* into English. Converted by Newman in 1846, Monteith dedicated his life and fortune to building the infrastructure of the Catholic community in the West of Scotland. All the religious orders were indebted to him: on the international scene he worked with the eccentric David Urquhart and Karl Marx, even taking a petition from the Armenian Church in Turkey asking the Pope to exercise moral leadership so that peace could be achieved worldwide. This was just before the definition of papal infallibility. It was all changed days from a hunted, hidden church.

## 93   The Free Kirk – and liberation theology before its time

Not many people would associate the 'wee frees' with liberation theology, the theology of the sixties and seventies in the twentieth century that has provided the springboard for seeing Christ as the one who came to free peoples in places such as South America and South Africa from oppression. *The Monthly Record* of the Free Church of Scotland fairly bristles when the subject of liberation theology is raised for it sees it as a left-wing subversion of the gospel truth, a destruction of Christ's divinity in the cause of presenting Him as a freedom fighter or political reformer. And yet from his comprehensive studies of the Free Church, Dr Donald Meek of the University of Edinburgh believes that the Free Kirk in the nineteenth century provides an early paradigm of the church-state critique and political pressure that is liberation theology.

The story begins with the alignment of church and state that brought about Reformation in Scotland. William of Orange's revolution settlement establishing Presbyterianism was the last in a long line of state decisions shaping and reshaping the Christian church in Scotland. It was always, however, a tense relationship. It became more tense after 1832 with the democratisation of the political system (and renewed biblical insights) leading to a campaign that kirks should be free to vote for and choose their ministers rather than have them imposed by landowners or burghs. The evangelical wing of the kirk cut its political teeth on the unsuccessful campaign for state money for church extension, the successful Chapels Act which gave the ministers of their beloved extension chapels the same status as the more regular ministers; and the Veto Act which promised at first to give congregations a veto over the ministers though it was eventually overturned. The walk-out in 1843 – the Disruption – was as much a political statement demanding that the state should comply with the kirk's wishes for an end to patronage as it was a religious movement: they voted with their feet against the landowners they hated.

When the Free Kirk that emerged from the Disruption lost its struggle to align the state with its views, it moved steadily to a more critical view of the state. In the nineteenth century, after the period of evictions and clearances that caused so much human suffering, when crofters began to agitate for land reform, they did so against the background of political teaching that was based on the study of the Old and to a lesser extent the New Testament. The Crofters' party in 1885 owed much to the Free Church for its impetus as did the achievement of the 1886 Crofters Holdings (Scotland) Act. On the other hand, the established church didn't approve and ministers who encouraged rebellion got into trouble. The Reverend Donald McCallum of Argyll was a stirring orator on behalf of the crofters and taught land questions from the Bible.

Union of the majority of the Free Church with other branches of the kirk left behind our present-day Free Church of Scotland. It moved steadily to reinforce the complete separation of the 'two kingdoms' of church and state but campaigns against the Sunday ferries in Lewis – and the direct action involved – reminded a lot of people that the 'wee frees' had still a great deal of political muscle to wield when they chose.

## 94   Sectarianism: the Rangers – Celtic variety!

Many would argue that sociology not theology lies behind most of the savagery that has disfigured the relationships between groups of Christians down through the ages. Those who would argue the thesis would find plenty of justification in the sectarian bitterness that emerged at the end of the last century and can be glimpsed still in the massed ranks of Rangers and Celtic football fans hurling quasi-religious abuse at one another from opposite ends of the terracing. It's a phenomenon that Edinburgh people like to think of as a Glasgow aberration but in fact the last 'No Popery' movement in Scotland arose in Edinburgh in the 1930s. The background was the emigration from Ireland in the nineteenth century of masses of cheap labour to fuel the Industrial Revolution. There were already sizeable numbers of the Irish in Britain but famine in the 1840s swelled these numbers dramatically. In Liverpool and Lancashire in the 1850s and 1860s there were spectacular anti-Irish riots, but here in Scotland the working classes – while also resenting the Irish working for lower wages than unionised labour – seemed to be more accepting of authority and more law-abiding, and so there were fewer riots. Dr Tom Gallagher, who wrote the study *Edinburgh Divided*, believes too that Scots were more secure in their Presbyterian faith and didn't see Catholicism as a real threat, as it was with the Anglo-Catholic movement in England.

Rangers Football Club emerged at the end of the nineteenth century from among the skilled workers who fiercely defended their exclusivity and their jobs for their sons by Freemasonry, the Orange Order and 'respectable' kirk membership. This supremacy was taken almost naturally into the area of recreation. Thus no Catholics. Soon afterwards, Celtic Football Club was set up by a Roman Catholic brother to raise money for destitute children. Although Protestants were involved from the start in Celtic, the two clubs represented two tribal factions in the working class and in particular in dockland. They represent sectarianism. In Edinburgh, Hibs emerged from a small Catholic immigrant community (a remarkable achievement) while Hearts originally received significant support from the Protestant skilled classes. Sectarianism in footballing Edinburgh, however, never attained the Glasgow proportions.

This makes all the more surprising the career of John Cormack who managed in the 1930s to have nine or ten councillors elected on a platform which blamed the 10 per cent Catholic population for all Edinburgh's ills: the unemployment of the thirties and a Scotland suffering from the decline in the empire. The mesmeric leader of Protestant Action hurled abuse weekly on the Mound, packed the Usher Hall several times a year and started street riots and court cases. In court he proudly declared 'one word from me and this street will flow with blood'. Older Edinburgh Catholics are still affected by the fear he inflicted on their community. Church of Scotland ministers said that his supporters were the 'churchless' but his activists were deeply religious. He himself came from a Baptist background and became hostile during the Irish War of Independence when he accused the priests of complicity with Sinn Fein. He was elected from Leith until the fifties and became a bailie. The blatant sectarianism he proclaimed in public is echoed on the present scene by people like Pastor Glass, except that they back their protest by appealing to Covenanting traditions. Despite individual kindness to Catholics, his campaign held back the movement towards Christian unity.

## 95 The Tory and Liberal parties at prayer

We've all heard the jibe that the Church of England is the Conservative party at prayer – although since David Jenkins became bishop of Durham, the Labour party seems to have staked its claim in England. In Scotland, the Church and Nation Report of the Church of Scotland in 1987 came out in the midst of an election campaign sounding like the Labour party manifesto. What then has been the relationship of the kirk to the political parties in Scotland?

The Whigs were the traditional derivatives of the Covenanters and so were strongly anti-Catholic and Presbyterian. The Tories were Episcopalian. When we come, however, to the second half of the nineteenth century, matters become more complex but we have more information. People signed for their vote and so we can see that United Presbyterian voters began with the Whigs and then moved to the Liberals. Free Kirk voters were Liberal and Auld Kirk voters Conservative. How this came about is fairly clear. The Auld Kirk supported patronage and so the landowners who benefited would appoint ministers who shared their conservative views. On the other hand, the Liberals crossed the class barrier. Their supporters tended to be poor but they stood for the extension of freedom and so they appealed to industrialists, many of whom paid the bills for Free Church expansion. Again by contrast, many of the poor belonged to the Auld Kirk because church extension made belonging to the Free Kirk an expensive business!

There were other intriguing line-ups. The Tories allied naturally with the brewers and the Auld Kirk. The Liberals identified with the Temperance Movement and so with the Free Church and United Presbyterian church. The United Presbyterian church was more sympathetic with trade unions and the working class, and so were strong in Glasgow.

The French Revolution brought a backlash of religiosity in

the country on the basis that if you could keep the masses contented by making them go to church then the revolutionary idea would disappear. Thomas Chalmers lived in dread of the anti-religious character of revolution and preached: 'If only people would listen to my social theories, revolution would be banished from the land.' And yet the only ministers who criticised the clearances were evangelicals like Chalmers. Chalmers' idea that 'whatever is, is right' gave way to reflection on how Knox was radical about society. Donald Smith, PhD, has spoken forcibly of the recovery of social criticism in the second half of the nineteenth century. John Glass of Greyfriars in the Auld Kirk was a friend of Keir Hardie and preached his ideas. Scott Matheson did similar work in the United Presbyterian church and James Begg of the Free Church was a remarkable and unusual combination of conservative theology and radical work for housing and the urban poor. Patrick Brewster of Paisley Abbey spoke at the Chartist rallies in the 1840s and was disciplined for it. James Barr in the 1920s took the process to its logical conclusion as an Independent Labour MP alongside Maxton and the Red Clydesiders while still a United Free Church minister. In Scotland then, the kirk has at times been conservative, but was never in danger of becoming the Tory party at prayer – or any other!

# THE CHURCH AND A CHANGING SOCIETY

## 96 A new age dawning

The nineteenth century was a time of accelerated change with the Industrial Revolution, the Highland Clearances and Irish immigration changing the shape of Scotland. Urbanisation brought diet, health and social problems; the rapid development of scientific knowledge was paralleled by a crisis in the church's confidence in how to draw guidance from the Bible when it seemed to be the product of so many literary forms; the state took over poor relief and eventually education too and this moved the church from the centre of people's lives to the side-lines; splits and reunions and the growth of Roman Catholicism destroyed the monolithic face of the kirk once and for all; and the increase of leisure, prosperity and mobility gave options to a church-centred weekend. A new age was dawning, and two world wars in the twentieth century destroyed the old pattern of life in unparalleled tragedy. A new age had dawned. Since Billy Graham's deceptive success in 1957, the church has spiralled in a seemingly unstoppable decline. There are many reasons for this but Professor T.C. Smout of the University of St Andrews suggests that one factor may well be that the church has failed to give a clear, continuing answer to the quintessential question: what happens next? The kirk seems irrelevant to a new age that is materialist and, despite the shadow of the bomb that could destroy this new age, has failed to point to the 'new age dawning' that is the essence of Christianity.

The new age dawning can be traced vividly in the OSA, the *Old Statistical Account* of the 1790s, then the NSA, the *New Statistical Account* of the 1840s, and the *Third Statistical Account* of the 1950s onwards, which is still continuing. The picture is clear of a church facing new problems and somewhat bewildered by the pace of change, yet clearly realising that the old ways just wouldn't do.

In the OSA, accounts of the two parishes of Monklands show

the dramatic impact of the Industrial Revolution: the need for new churches to serve the great town of Airdrie as it developed; alarm about the inability to pay a decent wage to the schoolmaster; and anxiety in West Monklands about the thirty inns or public houses. 'It is no uncommon thing for a labouring man to spend all his wages in these houses, and suffer his unhappy wife and children to continue in want and wretchedness' – and then the general observation: 'Trade produces affluence: affluence is the parent of luxury and dissipation, which infallibly undermine and dissolve the fabric.' Prophetic words for a drink, drugs and Aids-ridden second half of the twentieth century! The Bathgate account speaks of the famine of 1782: 'Not only the ordinary poor but the families of many labourers who were before decently supported must have perished with want without extraordinary assistance.' This realism is shown by Alexander (Jupiter) Carlyle, a leading Moderate and visionary author of the Inveresk account in 1792, as he argues comprehensively against those who object to a compulsory assessment now being necessary to support the poor. He too is well aware that without the right sort of building in the right place, the church will suffer in the new age. The Lochgelly account notes that 70 per cent of the church-goers were outside the established church, again a pointer to the end of the homogeneous character of the kirk that had been its strength *vis-à-vis* the state. The challenging side of the new age is put well at Dalmeny:

A spirit of enterprise and for rising in the world characterises the Scots in general: and this has so remarkably persuaded all ranks for these forty or fifty years past, that perhaps no people have in so short a period made so great advances in industry, agriculture, manufacture, refinement, public revenue and private wealth as the people of Scotland.

Could the kirk cope?
The NSA shows the population of an area like Dalkeith to be increasing steadily but that of areas like Monklands to be increasing by leaps and bounds. Thus Old Monkland in 1840:

The population of this parish is at present advancing at an amazing rate, and this prosperity is entirely owing to the coal and iron trade, stimulated by the discovery of the black band of ironstone, and the method of fusing iron by the hot blast. New villages are springing up almost every month and it is quite impossible to keep pace with the march of prosperity and the increase of the population.

There's clear evidence of strain on poor law provision and a presumption that concern should only be for the deserving poor. A contrast emerges: 'Among the agricultural part of the population, there is a great aversion to come on the poor's funds: they consider it degrading; but that spirit is almost extinct among the manufacturing and mining population.' Most ministers welcomed the prosperity but some questioned the effect on people's health of working in the new industries. 'In the country part of the parish, the people are in general strong and robust: but in Airdrie many of the weavers are feeble and small in stature' (New Monkland). Another significant factor for the church's future is its attitude to unions and strikes.

The frequent associations and combinations which prevail here, and are connected with similar combinations in different parts of the country, to raise the price of labour, are very hurtful. They interrupt trade, and attempt what is impracticable, as the price of all labour must be regulated by the demand. They keep trade's people in a constant state of agitation, and make them spend much of their time and money in attending their frequent meetings.

Whose side were they on? Frequent condemnations of alcohol tended to deepen the divide. Dalkeith is typical: 'the dram shops especially, that invite the labourer in the morning or minister to the cravings of street wanderers at night, ought to be regarded as a moral nuisance, and discountenanced by every person of respectability'. It's often not the condemnation but the way it is done!

The *Third Statistical Account* of the 1950s shows dramatically that the church is no longer the focus of the life of the community. People identify now with District or Region or parliamentary constituency rather than parish. We find Airdrie dominating the area in a way it never did before but we find churches rather than just 'the church'; they still have an important role but a much more marginal one. The population had continued to increase, but in a way that at times favoured Airdrie, and at others the landward area. The church had to cope. The minister in the fifties at Dalkeith was ambivalent but still optimistic. 'People do not seem to be any happier now than previously. Without doubt this is a restless and unquiet age.' Drink is again condemned – and materialism – but the church is still declared to be 'a power in town and country'. The main conclusion to the change is 'that the emphasis has shifted from the individual aspect of religion to the social'. The church hall has come into its own!

Headquarters of the Church of Scotland, Edinburgh

## 97 Sabbatarianism

'There they go to hell at a penny a mile.' The words were hurled by a fiery street preacher on 3 September 1865 at the departing rail passengers during what was known as the 'Sabbath War' of 1865, the attempt by Scottish evangelicals to stop the trains running on Sundays. It all began with the Reformers in 1560 who tried to impose a strict Jewish-style Sabbath on Scotland's Sundays and had such effect in first closing the shopping booths during the sermons and then extending the ban to Monday markets that the working week was reduced to five days and the commodity markets had to be relocated because of lack of space. As a result there was much resistance. The strict observance, however, didn't affect the Highlands until the end of the eighteenth century and began to ease away in Lowland Scotland after 1700. Then came the renewed attempt to impose the Sabbath by evangelicals in the nineteenth century as a response to the alienation of the working classes from church and to the tendencies in the middle classes to use the Sabbath for leisure purposes. Despite what we would now describe as the relatively large number of people going to church then (for example, one Sunday in Clydebank in 1893 56 per cent of the population was at church), the movement to re-establish the Sabbath, though initially successful, was ultimately a failure, apart from the areas in the remote Highlands and Islands which were dominated by the Free Church or some of the breakaway churches.

Two very different versions of a nineteenth-century Sabbath are worth noting. First, Professor Wallace, MP, editor of *The Scotsman*:

> There was scarcely anything that was safe to do . . . even during the meals, we were not to speak our own words or think our own thoughts. To me the day was a terror, it was so difficult to keep it perfectly, and I knew the doom of Sabbath-breakers.

On the other hand, John Younger in 1849 wrote that the Sabbath was

> The kindly interference of heaven with the stern conditions of our lot in the scale of humanity. There's no walk that a working man can take on the surface of his native earth like a walk to his place of worship. Here the harassments, the toils and anxieties of his everyday life appear as if cleared away before his footfall. Here he feels more certainly than at other times the true dignity of his own existence and ultimate destination.

Attempts to impose the Sabbath varied. A Dundee barber was condemned by the House of Lords (20 December 1837) because his apprentice shaved customers on the Sabbath. The Free Church prevented the opening of the Botanic Gardens on Sundays in 1862. The great battle, however, centred on the trains just as in the twentieth century it was to focus on the Skye ferry. In 1846, Sir Andrew Agnew, a Free Church elder, managed to turn a shareholders' meeting of the North British Railway into a theological debate over Sunday trains between Glasgow and Edinburgh. A 214,000-signature threat of boycott and the fourth commandment printed on the agenda won the day for a ban but on 3 September 1865 the trains were reinstated. Crowds gathered outside the station to hear Sunday trains being denounced but when Glasgow Presbytery of the Church of Scotland joined in, the prominent minister Norman McLeod of the Barony claimed that this was pharisaical. His views triumphed in most of Scotland but, even in 1985, there was much protest at a bank opening in Edinburgh on Sundays.

## 98    Drink and temperance

Drink and temperance are issues which have challenged the
Christian church since the early conflicts between Christ and
the Pharisees – even St Paul said we should take a little wine for
our stomach's sake. Drink can add to human celebrations, but it
can also make us avoid reality. Before the twentieth century
identified drink as destructive of human health and character,
Christians saw it as potentially corrupting yet still a good of
creation. One of the common caricatures of post-Reformation
Scotland is that it was sternly Calvinist and joyless yet the *First
Book of Discipline*, which covered all sins in great detail, had
nothing to say about drunkenness. The official account of the
second conversion of the earl of Huntly to Protestantism (he
died a Catholic eventually) tells of a weekend celebration by
town council and kirk session which began with a fast and ended
with a drunken orgy. One of the most famous ministers of the
eighteenth century, Dr Alexander Webster (1707-1784),
minister of the Tolbooth Church in Edinburgh, moderator and
compiler of the first national census of Scotland, was a high-
flying evangelical whose career prospered because of his
legendary drinking habits – his nickname was Dr Bonum
Magnum. In this he encapsulated a society in which drink in
large quantities was central to social interchange.

   The other side of the picture developed in the nineteenth
century and was most visible on the streets of the cities with
church congregations becoming increasingly shocked at the
men, women and children lying drunk in the gutter. The
statistics are staggering. Whisky had replaced ale as the drink of
the working classes. In Edinburgh there were 915 drink
licences issued in 1829, one for every fifteen families; in
Glasgow one for every fourteen. In one working-class parish in
Dundee there were eleven bakers' shops and 108 publicans in
1841. Tranent had fifty-two pubs while in Dundee there were
fifty-three – one pub to every eighty inhabitants. It was

estimated that the quantity of spirits consumed per head of population was seven pints a year in England, thirteen in Ireland and twenty-three in Scotland. By the mid-nineteenth century, the *Saturday Review* described the 'sons of the Covenanters' as 'the most drunken population on the face of the earth'. The poor drank in public, the rich in private.

Concern about the link with crime and concern about pubs being open on Sunday led to the Temperance Movement. The first temperance society in Scotland was founded at Maryhill, then a village outside Glasgow. By 1830 100 societies had been founded with a total membership of 15,000. John Dunlop, a Greenock solicitor and elder of the kirk, was possibly the founder of the Temperance Movement in Britain and William Collins, the publisher, brought out a periodical, *The Temperance Record*. With the coming from Ireland of Fr Theobald Matthew, Roman Catholics made common cause with evangelicals (though Bishop Gillis described them as 'spouting and talking societies'), with 40,000 processing on 17 July 1841. Splits, however, emerged between those who advocated restraint and those who demanded total abstinence. Some people were individually transformed but improvement in drink abuse only really came with excise duty and licensing laws in the twentieth century. Temperance has been described as the great failed reform movement of the nineteenth century.

## 99   A half-educated nation

Scotland's reputation for education has always been high but it
may still have managed to produce only a half-educated nation.
Since the church was in charge of education until 1872, and
largely influential for most of the years since, through its role on
the School Boards, the question of a half-educated nation is one
that has to be set against the Christian ideal of equality of
dignity and opportunity for all.

Before the Reformation, there were a number of different
kinds of schools, such as grammar schools and song schools,
both of which sent 'the lad o' pairts' on to the three universities
of St Andrews, Glasgow and Aberdeen. An Act of Parliament
of 1496 urged the nobility to educate their sons but John Major
in the 1520s had criticised their slowness to respond. The *First
Book of Discipline*, the blueprint of the Reformation, had more
to say about education (mainly concerning the universities)
than any other subject and is a landmark in its ideal of a school
in every parish. It's doubtful, however, if more than half of
Scotland's parishes had a school before the Education Act of
1696. By 1700, 85 per cent of craftsmen and tradesmen could at
least sign their names but only 50 per cent of servants and
labourers, and the proportions ranged downwards from urban
Scotland through the rural lowland areas to the Highlands. In
1818, a report of the General Assembly found that in Uist less
than 400 of a population of 5,000 could read: and real crisis
developed in the urban slums. Only 7 per cent of the children in
the Gorbals were at school in 1842 and in 1846, and only 46 per
cent of the children in Glasgow as a whole.

The nineteenth century saw the church beginning to lose
ground in its 'supreme and exclusive right to educate'. Despite
the Ragged Schools and efforts from Thomas Guthrie to
educate the poor and despite 292,000 children attending
Sunday school by 1851, society also came to see education more
and more as ideally far more secular than the sort of education

described by John Mitchell in 1780: to learn the catechism then was quite sufficient. The Disruption of 1843 led to the Free Church duplicating parish schools but also to the loss of many schoolmasters in their recruitment of new ministers. There were now nine or ten different types of schools, under different patrons, and there were more private schools than all the parish schools put together in both the old kirk and the Free Church. These private schools and the practice of the upper classes in having their children educated in England contradict the myth that in Scotland the gentry and the peasants were educated side by side. Even the middle classes, who went to the same schools as the poor, attended school for very much longer and there the divisions arose. None the less, it is to the credit of Scottish education that far more working-class children went to university in Scotland both before and particularly after the Reformation (even though they mainly took arts and set their sights on school teaching). The Education Act of 1872 handed over all the schools to new School Boards but since they were still dominated by the ministers, Catholics kept their own schools while still paying for state schools in their taxes. These they handed over in 1918 in return for the Catholic character of their schools being preserved. Only one question was left: could the state do better for the 'half-educated nation?' Clearly in terms of material resources, it did – but in other areas?

New College and Free Church College, Edinburgh

## 100   The poverty debate

The clearest characteristic of Christ's teaching is his identification with the poor. Perhaps the greatest question mark against the history of Scottish Christian religion is whether it failed the poor by introducing the concept of the 'deserving poor' in recent centuries. Did it stem from a return to the Old Testament where poverty was seen as a sign of God's displeasure? Be that as it may, we can see with the benefit of hindsight a contradictory tension in the ideals of the Scottish Reformers which was to burst into open debate in the church of the nineteenth century. On the one hand there is the stirring 'Beggars' Summons' posted at the door of friaries throughout Scotland in 1559, a demand from 'the blynd, cruked, beddrelles, wedowis, orphelingis, and all uther pure, sa viseit be the hand of God, as may not worke' for restitution of wrongs past and reformation for the future. On the other hand, the *First Book of Discipline* went on to see care of the poor as a Christian duty but immediately added 'we are not patrons for stubborn and idle beggars who, running from place to place, make a craft of their begging, whom the civil magistrate ought to punish'. Raising the money for this poor relief caused massive problems with eight schemes in as many years failing in Edinburgh. In 1574, Parliament gave local authorities power to raise a compulsory poor rate but this proved to be immensely unpopular so the kirk session – which was landed with the problem by 1600 – resorted to all sorts of choices. In Aberdeen a virtually guaranteed income for poor relief came from fines for fornication, but elsewhere money was raised by raffles and bazaars.

The nineteenth-century debate centred in the twenty-five years up to 1844 on whether there should be a compulsory assessment in place of the voluntary system. The established church maintained it was adequate and that the able-bodied poor were not helped by handouts. They should be encouraged to change their lives. Thomas Chalmers attempted small parish care of the poor in St John's in Glasgow in the 1820s by breaking down the parish into units. Careful analysis showed, however, that his poor relief touched only a fraction of the urban poor. Andrew Thomson, James Begg and McGill, one of Chalmers' associates at the Tron, took a different line and Dr W.P. Allison, an Episcopalian professor of medicine at the University of Edinburgh, openly debated the issue with Chalmers. His argument that a legal provision for all the poor could alone meet the problem won the day in the Poor Law Act of 1845.

The 'Christian Socialists' continued in the 1890s and 1900s to make poverty an ethical issue but the established churches – with later exceptions such as Lord George MacLeod of Fuinary – hesitated from positive alignment. In the 1930s, thousands of members were alienated by the kirk's insistence on church dues. In the Catholic community, the voluntary work of the St Vincent de Paul society was balanced by the emergence of Socialists like John Wheatley. In the post-war development of the welfare state, the kirk's role was on the side-lines. In complete contrast, its voluntary social work remained massive and innovative. The 1980s saw the government encouraging the voluntary response to poverty again: the kirk responded by denouncing the cuts and redoubling its caring outreach with dwindling numbers of mainly middle-class members. Can the kirk get it right for the poor this time?